THE MANAGER'S POCKET GUIDE TO
CREATIVITY

Alexander Hiam

D0907685

HRD PRESS
Amherst, Massachusetts

LAKEWOOD PUBLICATIONS
Minneapolis, Minnesota

Published by:

HRD Press
22 Amherst Road
Amherst, MA 01002
1-800-822-2801
413-253-3490 (fax)
www.hrdpress.com

Lakewood Publications
50 South Ninth Street
Minneapolis, MN 55402
1-800-707-7769
612-340-4819 (fax)
www.trainingsupersite.com

 PRINTED IN CANADA

ISBN 0-87425-436-1

Cover design by Eileen Klockars
Editorial services by Mary George

TABLE OF CONTENTS

INTRODUCTION

Reinvent the Wheel?
No Thanks—Haven't Got the Time

PEOPLE OFTEN USE THE EXPRESSION "Let's not reinvent the wheel" when they want to ensure that time and energy isn't wasted on needless work. Why spend time revising a whole line of products when only one product needs improving? Or why spend energy re-designing your customer service function when you can benchmark most of it from another company? Why do anything all over again, from the very beginning, when a few adjustments will give you the results you need?

But there is another, hidden aspect of the idiom "reinvent the wheel." I'm referring to **how** we do productive things, not **what** we do.

It struck me recently that the invention of the modern-day wheel must have taken an awfully long time, and upon doing some research, I learned it had in fact taken many thousands of years. To be precise, developing the wheel from its first crude version—a cross section of a tree trunk with a bored-out hole—into its basic modern-day form—a flexible rim with spokes running to a solid hub—took four and a half thousand years, from 5000 BC to 500 BC. The lengthy invention process we humans went through was, let's face it, anything but efficient. And if left to our own devices, we generally solve creative problems at the same plodding speed with which we invented the wheel.

Needless to say, none of us have thousands of years to discover solutions to such problems, to see what should have been obvious from the start. But let's not even take **one** year. Let's improve our natural thought processes to such a degree that we can invent "wheels"—whatever we may need—in minutes instead of millennia. It can be done if we realize that **how** we go about inventing, imagining, and creating is the key to what we come up with and how quickly we come up with it.

What I have to offer in this book, and what the field of corporate creativity has to offer in general, is the chance to improve upon the natural process of creative thought—to bring innovation to **how** we think, not just what we think—and thereby cut dramatically the cycle time for generating state-of-the-art solutions. Is there a secret to creativity? Yes: thinking in new ways. It is a secret all of us can discover and use, both for ourselves and for our organizations.

About This Pocket Guide

YOU WILL FIND IN THIS GUIDEBOOK an approach to creativity that offers practical tools and suggestions for creative thinking while never losing touch with an essential component of that thinking: its looseness, its freedom, its risk taking. To gain new insights into any subject, we must "get unstuck"—we must view the subject in a new light. And that includes the topic of creativity itself.

As you will see in this guidebook, and as explained in the preview below, the practical elements of "doing" creative thinking—the methods that help us get un-stuck—can themselves be creative. In fact, what better way to drive home the power of the creative thought process than to go out on a limb and **be creative about creativity**? That's what this book does, and what you will soon be doing too.

A creative approach is just one of the many features that sets this book apart. My goal is to inspire you in order to help you achieve breakthrough thinking. It's going to be fun, so let's get started!

WHAT TO EXPECT: A QUICK PREVIEW

1. A Personal Creativity Assessment

Are you creative? Of course, because **everyone** is capable of creative thinking. But it is immensely revealing to look closely at the many **barriers** to and **enablers** of creativity and see which ones apply to you. Doing so not only allows you to gauge how creative your work-

> ▶ See
> Chapter 1

place behavior is right now, but also helps you identify **how to make it more creative**. And if you supervise or train others, you can use this assessment to understand what you must do to help them sustain creative thinking in their work. So go ahead, take the creativity test. You have nothing to lose and a lot to gain.

2. A Look at Ways We Close Off Creativity

This is where I rant and rave about the terrible, stupid things we all do, to ourselves and our workplaces, to block creative thinking. Because there are some very simple, basic issues we need to work on, issues that crop up repeatedly in the organizations I

> ▶ See
> Chapters 2 & 4

visit or consult with. Fixing them is the "no-brainer" approach to creativity, but only if you take notice of them in the first place. So please review the checklist you will find in Chapter 2, to ensure that you and your associates aren't making any of these commonplace errors. It's not enough to learn creative thinking methods and then employ them; you also have to identify and destroy behaviors that smother creative thinking!

3. A Realistic, Useful Creativity Process

Sometimes it is helpful to follow a "thought map" designed to lead you through the entire creative thinking process. There are many such guides in print today, some presented as problem-solving methods and others

See CHAPTER 3

as creative-process aids. But they don't really work because they fail to provide any insight into, or instruction on, their core activity: thinking creatively. They just label one of the steps something like "Generate Ideas" and leave it to you to figure out how to actually carry out the step. Worse, some applications make their first step "Define the Problem," when in truth it's often devilishly hard to achieve enough insight just to realize there is a problem worth thinking about.

Consequently, I've included a new and better model of the creativity process, one that will help you find subjects for creative thinking and then make real headway on those subjects. All the creative thinking methods in this book can be applied to the process. Basically, if you get stuck on any process step, pick the creativity method applicable to that step and use it to get unstuck (most methods work anywhere, but check my notes in the text). Sounds simple, and it is.

4. Personal and Group-Facilitation Aids

I call these useful practices and strategies "the building blocks of creativity," and they come in many different shapes and sizes. You can piece them together to form your own creative process, or tailor them to the specific needs of the training group you're working with. You can also use them on a personal level, as a way to break uncreative habits in your daily workplace routine.

▶ See CHAPTER 5

5. Creative Thinking Methods

These are the process tools that help you "do" creative thinking. They are similar to brainstorming (the one tool I think everyone knows), but they work a lot better. I designed all of them, though not from scratch and not just for this book. They reflect lots of study and experience, and I've seen them produce good results for both individuals and groups.

▶ See CHAPTERS 6 TO 12

6. Applied Creativity, Not Games

One way in which my methods differ from others out there in the world of creativity consulting is that they are designed for practical application. I focus squarely on real-world subjects, things you need creative ideas about **now**. Even in training events, I favor rolling up one's sleeves and getting engaged in pressing issues,  **A Notable Feature** the questions and problems at hand, since there are so many of them at any time in the average workplace.

I've noticed that most people prefer this direct kind of approach—would rather dig into their actual concerns than do what seem like (and often are) silly training activities. And from what I've seen, people get much more out of real-world, applied creative thinking than out of puzzles and games. So I now use such activities only as warm-ups in my consulting and training. Puzzles and games might be fun, sure, but it's more important for people to increase their creativity by focusing on real-world issues of value to them and their organizations.

7. Training Transfer Assessment

Whether you use this book independently for personal education or as part of a training program, you won't See CHAPTER 13 benefit from anything you learn unless you can **transfer it to the workplace**. The best way to ensure transferal is to focus this book's methods on your actual, pressing creativity needs at work. I've included tools that will help you take this important step, that come equipped with a necessary real-world focus. They form my basic contribution to transferal.

However, if transferal is a problem in your workplace, you probably will need extra help. To give you a hand, I've included an assessment instrument in Chapter 13. Use it to identify the barriers to transferal; then make it your personal project to chip away at them.

8. New Stuff—Lots of New Stuff

Every one of the above "deliverables" is itself novel and creative, reflecting my conviction that there is no point reiterating tired wisdom on a topic, **especially** if the topic is creativity. I've rethought almost

⊛ A Notable Feature

every aspect of creativity, and I can honestly say that this book is radically different from anything that's previously appeared on the topic, even my own work.

Which means that if this is your first book on creativity, you should find it intuitive, clear, and powerful, and you should feel empowered to dig right in and start thinking creatively at work (and at home) right away. And if this is a repeat visit to the topic, you should also see immediate benefits as you discover new and better tools and techniques for creative thinking.

9. My Own Creative Thinking

I really hate books that tell you what to do instead of **showing** you. Mastery of a skill should be a requirement for teaching it; yet in creativity training sessions and books, mastery of creative thinking is rarely shown. I think I know why: such thinking is loose and uninhibited, and thus can be embarrassing if taken out of context.

We are all far more willing to publicize the carefully developed end-result of a creative thought process than to demonstrate the process itself. But in the real world, people learn creative thinking best when it is **modeled** for them. So the mix needs to be weighted far more toward the showing than the telling.

In writing this book, I set aside my fears of embarrassment and shared many of my own thought processes, including examples based on my personal mental maps and scripts. Some of the ideas I offer may be  absurd, but in creative thinking you frequently have to generate lots of out-there ideas to find any gems (for example, NEC Corporation's New Ventures program evaluates 55 employee ideas for each one it funds). I've never written as potentially embarrassing a book as the one you're reading right now, but then again, I've never written a book as useful to my readers either.

Well, that concludes the quick preview of what you can expect to find in the guidebook. Now read Part One, which explains the fundamentals of creative thinking, or, if you are in a hurry for a creative solution, simply thumb through the book, pick a method that's likely to work, and then try it. And as Yoda, from the *Star Wars* movies, might say were he in charge of developing a creativity curriculum:

> May the force of creativity be with you!

(Hmm . . . I wonder what a *Star Wars* creativity course would be like. Maybe that should be my next project. Nah, forget it, I must be nuts. But it's always worth considering a new idea, no matter **how** silly, right?)

 PART ONE
The Fundamentals

1

Assessing Personal Creativity

I TEND TO BE A CONTRARIAN, and so I guess it
shouldn't surprise me to find that my view of creativity
is just about the opposite of the one that dominates in
corporate training and consulting today. My view is
that creativity is an individual sport at heart, not a
team sport. Sure, it is often necessary, and sometimes
even helpful, to work on creative projects with teams or
other groups. But even when a group is convened, the
bottom line is that ideas have to come from the fertile
imaginations of individual group members. If you don't
have at least one "idea person" in the group, it will
fail. And so my approach to creativity is individual-
istic—I'm convinced the key is to increase the level of
creativity of the individuals in any organization.

Yet many consultants and trainers seem to focus on group
processes as the key to creativity. That's all well and
good, and I agree that group processes can be run in ways
that maximize individual creativity. But it is important to keep in mind that the groups are made up of individuals—individuals who are more or less creative,
depending upon their training, preparation, and other

factors such as their work environment and whether their supervisors encourage or stifle their creativity.

Individuals—more or less creative individuals. That's the key to corporate creativity. And in most organizations, individuals are less creative rather than more. They are certainly less creative than they could be, and less creative than they need to be if their employers are to thrive in a turbulent, challenging business environment.

VISUALIZING YOUR CREATIVITY

Exhibit 1, on the following page, presents a beautiful photograph by noted photographer Ken Kipen. It is a fine creative work in its own right. But I include it here because it is also a wonderful visual metaphor for individual creativity. Before we get to a more "technical" approach to individual creativity, I want to spend a few minutes with you examining this image and using it to help you visualize your own creativity.

The photograph's subject is a greenhouse—one that has obviously been deserted for some time. Little grows inside it, as presumably nobody waters the parched soil of what, at one time, was probably a thriving garden. But outside, and clamoring to get in, is a tangled mass of weeds and vines. The door is ajar, and one can easily

EXHIBIT 1. "Greenhouse Ruin" by Ken Kipen

5

imagine entering it and doing the simple things that bring a garden back to life—planting, watering, and tending it. Many seeds from the weeds and vines must have found their way inside over the years, and must be waiting dormant for conditions to improve.

To me, this greenhouse represents the imagination of most individuals in the workplace. Unless you happen to work in a creative profession, you probably haven't cultivated this greenhouse for many years. And yet it is still there, and the door is ajar. In a sense, the goal of this book is to bring this greenhouse back to life.

To extend the metaphor a little further, it is also interesting to think about **how** someone might cultivate the greenhouse garden. With a neat planting of one species, everything in well-weeded rows? That image is often the first one to spring to people's minds, but it isn't a particularly helpful one. For in this greenhouse, the plants represent ideas, and a row of identical ideas is of no value to someone who seeks creativity.

Instead, the gardener needs to encourage those eager weeds and vines to enter the door and take up residence. A rich, diverse, tangled growth of ideas is just the thing for this greenhouse! And if you cultivate it well, giving your ideas the nutrients they need, and sheltering them from the harmful extremes of the environment outside, then your greenhouse will sustain a riotous growth of ideas, ready for harvesting whenever you need them.

But how well does your garden of ideas grow right now? Is it a repetitive row of commonplace thoughts, or, even worse, a barren bed of dusty soil? Does your greenhouse provide enough protection from the harsh extremes of your work environment to allow ideas to mature? Do you water and seed the garden with sufficient attention and care?

Such questions are highly provocative—that's the beauty of a rich visual metaphor. But they need to be translated into hard-nosed, fact-based information if we are to act upon them. So now I'd like to switch gears again, setting this greenhouse metaphor aside in order to show you how to make a practical assessment of the current state of your own, individual creativity.

Assessing YOUR CREATIVITY

The Question: Are You Creative?

Most people read the above question as "Are you an inherently creative person, an artist by temperament, full to overflowing with fresh, imaginative, zany ideas?" Please don't read it that way.

7

The problem is, most of us think this question addresses the presence or absence of some rare gift—a gift that is far more common among artists than people in the average workplace. Not so!

When I ask you if you are creative, I am simply asking something about your **behavior**. Do you behave in ways that are creative, ways that can lead you to generate many fresh ideas, to offer those ideas to others, and to apply them in the context of work? If so, then you're creative. If not, then you aren't, even if you think you have a naturally creative temperament.

Remember, anyone can be creative. It's just a natural set of behaviors we can all engage in. So please read my opening question as you would the question "Are you a parent?" If your answer is no today, you can still be a parent someday in the future. We all have within us the essential abilities we need to take on a parental role. Similarly, we all have the essence of creativity within us. We're talking about basic, core behaviors, things that are part of what makes us human. It's not rocket science. It's just creativity.

So, let's start again. Are you creative?

I hope your initial, pat answer (whether yes or no) has now been replaced by a thoughtful "Hmm. Let me think

8

about it." Because that is a much more useful response. And now I'm going to show you an even better way to think about that question and your response to it.

Personal Barriers and Enablers

The extent to which any individual behaves creatively is a direct result of two factors:

1. Personal **barriers** to creativity
2. Personal **enablers** of creativity

Therefore, a great way to assess anyone's creativity is to ask a bunch of questions that help the person identify his or her barriers and enablers.

In the average workplace, employees tend to be blocked from creativity by a variety of personal barriers. They also tend to have few personal enablers. Combine the two conditions, and you have a creativity deficit. (If you're thinking "Not me," or "Not in my organization," think again, because I come across this problem in nearly every organization I visit as a consultant, trainer, and author.) The purpose of this guidebook is to help you, as an individual worker **or** as a manager or trainer of other workers, **to reduce the creativity deficit in your workplace**. And a great place to start is by assessing the barriers and enablers affecting you and those around you. I've come up with a useful tool designed to help you do just that: the Personal Creativity Assessment.

9

About the Assessment Questions

Before you move on to the assessment, let me provide you with a brief explanation of my approach to this tool and others in the guidebook.

I develop commercial assessments and surveys for the Human Interactions Assessment & Management line of products, which is marketed to corporate trainers by HRD Press. Many of those products contain carefully validated questions that, to prevent biased responses, are written and organized in such a way that users cannot guess what we are measuring. But a less formal, more informative style of assessment sometimes works out better, particularly when assessments are designed for educational use, like the ones in this book are.

In such cases, I like to lay all my cards on the table. You will thus find that this assessment, like others in the guidebook, makes very clear what each question is about. For example, questions about personal barriers to creativity are labeled as such rather than mixed with other questions; each question is clearly labeled so you know what factor it measures; and each question is worded to inform rather than mislead, so you can also use the assessment as a checklist when working on crea-tivity issues. This approach may not be as scientific as others, but given our special purposes here, it is more helpful and educational.

10

THE PERSONAL CREATIVITY ASSESSMENT

Instructions: Simply check off all the statements that apply to you; then refer to the interpretation guides that follow the checklists. Later, you will be given a creativity matrix on which to plot your assessment results.

✓ PERSONAL ENABLERS

☐ **Knowledge.** I am aware of many practical techniques for generating ideas.

☐ **Locus of control.** I am empowered to be creative by a sense of control over my personal circumstances and fate when at work.

☐ **Confidence.** I am confident of my ability to produce valuable new ideas and solutions.

☐ **Open-mindedness.** I am drawn to new perspectives, even when they clash with my assumptions or values.

☐ **Experience.** I have often benefited from my own and others' creativity in past work experiences.

☐ **Role models.** There are a number of people in my workplace who have succeeded in part because of their high level of creativity.

☐ **Leadership support.** My leaders (including supervisors and managers) encourage creativity.

☐ **Leadership openness.** My leaders are open to input and enjoy listening to my ideas.

(Continued)

11

THE PERSONAL CREATIVITY ASSESSMENT (Continued)

✓ MORE PERSONAL ENABLERS

☐ **Rewards.** People who exhibit creativity in my workplace are rewarded for their efforts

☐ **Training.** We receive plenty of good training to help us be more creative.

☐ **Emotional resiliency.** I feel secure enough in my workplace to handle the risks of creativity.

☐ **Diverse inputs.** My work and hobbies expose me to a wide variety of ideas and practices.

☐ **Independence.** I am viewed as an independent thinker by my peers.

☐ **Lack of attachment.** I am not attached to specific ideas or theories; I like exploring many alternatives.

☐ **Playfulness.** I like "fooling around" with ideas, and find creative thinking and problem-solving activities fun.

☐ **Persistence.** Once I get thinking about a problem, I don't set it completely aside until I've solved it—even if it takes many weeks.

☐ **Empathy.** I am good at sensing what others think and feel, and this skill helps me pick up or add to the good ideas of my associates.

(Continued)

THE PERSONAL CREATIVITY ASSESSMENT (Continued)

✓ MORE PERSONAL ENABLERS

❑ **Self-perception.** I see myself as a creative person.

❑ **Inventiveness.** I like to invent new products and devices.

❑ **Boundary-breaking.** I often come up with fresh ideas by making connections between unrelated things or unrelated activities.

Interpretation Guide — Personal Enablers

Add up the check marks to see the number of personal enablers you have right now. The more you have, the more likely you are to be successfully creative at work. If you checked 11 or more statements, then you can classify yourself as having a high level of enablers.

✓ PERSONAL BARRIERS

❑ **Acceptance.** I tend to take a "don't rock the boat" attitude instead of challenging the status quo.

❑ **Low self-evaluation of work.** I don't think the work I do in my job is particularly valuable or worthwhile in the grand scheme of things.

❑ **Lack of skill diversity.** My work requires a specific, narrow set of skills.

❑ **Limited chances for skill development.** My work does not give me many opportunities to develop new skills.

(Continued)

13

THE PERSONAL CREATIVITY ASSESSMENT (Continued)

✓ MORE PERSONAL BARRIERS

☐ **No challenges.** My work does not challenge me.

☐ **No sense of personal responsibility.** I don't feel personally responsible for the results of my work because it's hard to see how my own contributions affect overall performance.

☐ **Limited size of solution sets.** We are encouraged to solve problems in certain ways, rather than to explore unconventional approaches.

☐ **No role models.** Most of the time, my supervisors do not act or think like creative people.

☐ **Narrow-minded peer acceptance.** My work associates are not open to new or wild ideas.

☐ **Sanctions.** People who spend too much time on creative thinking are labeled as trouble-makers or accused of being lazy.

☐ **Fears.** I don't like to contribute too many ideas, because if people think you're a trouble-maker, things will go badly for you in the long run.

☐ **Personal narrow-mindedness.** I guess I'm fairly set in my ways. My feeling is, "If it ain't broke, don't fix it."

(Continued)

THE PERSONAL CREATIVITY ASSESSMENT (Continued)

✓ MORE PERSONAL BARRIERS

☐ **Bipolar thinking.** I generally prefer to look at two alternatives—that's why I often find myself thinking in in terms of "either/or" solutions.

☐ **Overconfidence.** At work, we're pretty certain that our approach is the right one—maybe so certain that we don't always examine alternatives as well as we could.

☐ **Time pressures.** There is so much pressure to finish one thing and get to the next that I rarely have time to take a thoughtful, lengthy approach to a problem.

☐ **Procedure constraints.** I have some ideas about how to do things better, but I don't bring them up because they would violate our policies and procedures.

☐ **Red tape.** There isn't much point in contributing creative ideas, because they will just get lost in the bureaucracy.

☐ **Close-minded leaders.** My leaders (supervisors, managers) are not very open to new ideas. They tend to react defensively.

☐ **Group-process constraints.** I'd like to do more creative thinking, but there isn't much opportunity for it in the way we run our meetings and projects.

(Continued)

15

THE PERSONAL CREATIVITY ASSESSMENT (Concluded)

✓ **MORE PERSONAL BARRIERS**

☐ **Conformance pressure.** If you don't look and act the "right" way, you can't succeed in my workplace.

Interpretation Guide — Personal Barriers

Add up the check marks to see the number of personal barriers you have right now. Less is more for this scale, as the fewer barriers you have, the more likely you are to be successfully creative at work. If you checked 11 or more statements, then you can classify yourself as facing a high level of barriers in your job. **Any** barrier is a potential problem, though; so the best scores are in the 0-to-3 range.

Overall Interpretation of the Assessment

Once again, are you creative? And are your associates or employees creative? Now that you are familiar with the assessment tool, you have a powerful, detailed approach to answering these questions.

For starters, you can readily classify yourself or others according to the levels of enablers and barriers revealed by the assessment. Then you can focus on details by identifying which barriers are present (these become targets for removal) and which enablers are not (these become targets for inclusion in the workplace over the coming weeks and months).

But don't forget the simplest answer to both these questions—which, for just about everyone, is "Sort of." That is, based on this assessment, we all tend to be "sort of creative." It's not a straightforward yes or no answer, because nobody can check all the enablers and leave all the barriers blank, or vice versa. And that means—if you are an optimist—that everyone who completes the assessment can answer yes to some extent when asked "Are you creative?"

Now keep your "optimist hat" on for another moment (metaphors are a building block of creativity, so I use them as often as possible). If, considering the assessment results, you view the "creativity glass" as half full (yes, that's another metaphor, I know), then you can't help but regard what's in the glass as a valuable resource, something rich and deeply satisfying just waiting to be consumed. And so you also should consider the simple approach of **building on existing enablers**—both your own and those of others.

Take another look at your responses to the "Personal Enablers" section of the assessment (and don't forget to look again at your employees' or trainees' responses if you handed out the tool). Each check mark represents a wonderful resource, a little spark of creativity you can grow into a flame simply by exposing it to the air (love those metaphors).

For example, if you have positive role models for creative behavior, you can use them to encourage creative behavior in yourself and others. All you have to do is give them the charge of modeling creative behavior and then make sure work schedules expose others to them in creative problem-solving contexts. For instance, this might be as simple as "planting" creative people in new quality improvement teams for short periods of time.

Always keep in mind that each enabler offers you a powerful lever for stimulating creative behavior and overcoming the barriers to creativity (to restate a key point by using a new metaphor).

The Personal Creativity Matrix

You can also visualize anyone's workplace creativity by plotting the results of the assessment on the Personal Creativity Matrix. It isn't difficult—simply use the number of check marks in each category (enablers and barriers) to find your position on the categories' numeric lines (0 to 20). Move into the matrix from those two points until you reach the point of intersection. You'll end up in one of the four matrix cells and get a clear idea of where you stand in relation to creativity. (Note that trainers or managers who have given the assessment tool to a group can also use the matrix to plot the average score of the group.)

EXHIBIT 2. Personal Creativity Matrix

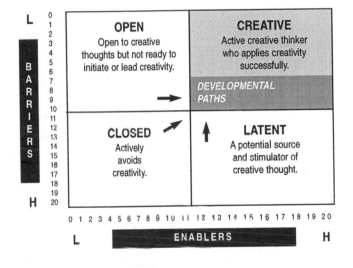

Let's say you plot your scores and find you aren't in the most desirable portion of the matrix—the upper right-hand cell, where high-quality creative thought is easily attainable at work. Don't despair! Very few of the factors we measured in the assessment are immutable—perhaps none are (psychologists have debated the durability of such personality variables). So you can take steps to improve the scores, for yourself or anyone you supervise or train. It is quite feasible to boost the strength and number of personal enablers. And it is also perfectly feasible to reduce the barriers to creativity.

For many of us, simply having this list of our enablers and barriers helps us begin to take control over them! So please view your creativity profile as a work in progress. Assume you will move "up and out" over time.

Protecting Personal Creativity in the Workplace

Another absolutely vital caveat: the profiles are only part of the creativity equation. They concern natural tendencies—how easily and often we think and act creatively. But such tendencies can be undermined, by us or others, through uncreative actions or processes—things that destroy the fragile growth within our creativity greenhouse. In Chapters 2 and 4, I examine the all-too-common ways in which our creativity can be smothered by organizational culture and rituals, inappropriate supervisory styles, and our own bad habits.

Uncreative Habits
Nine Ways We Close Off Creativity

LET'S BE BRUTALLY HONEST. It's easy to blow creativity big time by making simple errors that stifle creativity or allow the fruits of creative thinking to spoil on the tree. And most people do. Yet much of the advice you get on creativity is so sophisticated that it fails to address these commonplace errors. For instance, the details of how to run a group brainstorming process are, in truth, of little consequence if you hardly ever brainstorm in the first place.

I'm often asked to come into an organization as a consultant or trainer to help people "get out of the box" and find new solutions. Whether it's new product concepts, new business strategies, or new ways to cut errors or improve employee performance, I am usually surprised to find I can suggest many novel approaches. Surprised because, when you come right down to it, I'm not necessarily smarter than my clients, and I rarely know their industry as well as they do. So why do I see all sorts of alternatives they don't? Because they are failing to "do" creativity in the first place. They are making some of those obvious errors that trap you in routine thinking and close off creative avenues—even creative avenues that seem fairly obvious to most outsiders.

I'm not the only one who feels this way. I often talk to employees who know precisely what their organization's problems are, and how to solve them, but find their senior managers are quite unable to see the obvious. And customers often offer brilliant insights when given half a chance—brilliant to management, but painfully obvious to customers!

"On my count now, transform yourselves into creative, free-thinking mavericks. Ready?"

These sorts of experiences have led me to believe that a foundational attack on the corporate creativity problem is sometimes more valuable than the sophisticated "upper story" approaches taken by most experts. As a result, I have gradually compiled a list of the most common "no-brainer" errors, things that routinely block creativity in organizations, and for many of us as individuals as well. The resulting list might be called "Creativity for Dummies," except the reality is, we **all** make these dumb mistakes, and far too often. They are embedded in our organizational cultures and in our individual training as students and employees. They may even have some value under circumstances in which creativity is not required. But the vast majority of us live and work in circumstances that demand creativity, and so we all need to jettison these bad habits. Now.

THE NINE BAD HABITS

1. Failure to Ask Questions

Creativity requires an inquisitive mind. Fresh, creative thoughts don't grow in the dry soil of mindless acceptance. Yet it is easy to go through one's day without calling anything important into question. If we would only deliberate on business decisions as carefully as we do on what to order from a restaurant menu, we would effortlessly become far more creative.

Unless you ask lots of **why** questions, you won't generate creative insights. Period. To avoid this most common of creativity errors, be sure to peek under all the carpets, including your own. Don't take anything for granted. Especially success.

To put this principle into action, we need to get in the **good** habit of asking ourselves and those around us to

23

question more things, more often. If you aren't sure how to do this, just spend a little time with a four-year-old. Children around this age not only question **you** relent-lessly (why **is** the sky blue, anyway?), but also question their **environment** by constantly manipulating it (what happens if you try to stack these blocks really high? Oh, they fall down. Hmm. Wonder what happens if they fall on Dad's coffee mug. Cool, it breaks!). Or if you haven't got anyone in that age group handy, try watching a teenager explore a new software program. Kids at this age do the same thing: "poke" something every way they can to find out how it works. And in the process, they surface many relationships that adults wouldn't discover unless equipped with a user's manual.

When was the last time you "poked" your own work processes in the same way a kid does a new computer game? Hard to remember, isn't it? That means you're not asking those loosely defined, impulsive questions that so often give birth to creative insight.

Don't feel bad—you're not alone. The failure to ask questions is a widespread social phenomenon; in fact, most of our social institutions seem designed to limit, if not outright discourage, creative enquiry. And many of the processes used in organizations are just as bad, if not worse. Take the typical staff meeting, the most blatant example of an **un**creative process.

At every staff meeting I attend or see transcripts of, its leader unwittingly **fails to ask for creative ideas**, even at the most opportune points. A formal, professional atmosphere is combined with a structured conversation path or meeting agenda to keep people "on track," or "focused." Great. I too hate meetings that drag on and on. But I also hate meetings in which no freewheeling occurs. Why meet in the first place if you don't take advantage of the group's unique creative potential? One person's question or comment can easily stimulate another's imagination—**if** you ask for imaginative thinking. Thus no business meeting should reach its end without the leader asking for creative ideas. (We'll return to this topic later, in Chapter 4, and take a further look at encouraging creativity in meetings.)

So now that you're aware of this uncreative habit, you can start rattling its chains. Try looking at the world through more inquisitive eyes; try getting ideas in motion; try asking the all-important question: **"Why?"** See what happens!

2. Failure to Record Ideas

Oh boy, this is a really big one. I can't tell you the number of times I've worked through some horribly complex problem-solving process with a client, finally come up with a solution that works, and then heard somebody say, "Hey, now that you mention it, didn't we look at that alternative a few years ago?" Great. Then why did it take a crisis and a major two-month team effort to regenerate the idea? Because nobody had recorded it in a usable form.

I recently attended a new-product ideation retreat with an employee group from a large, mature consumer-products company. The event was part of a long, costly effort to find a dozen concepts worthy of test marketing—a goal that required generating hundreds of ideas. During a break, one company veteran told me, "As I listen to all these new ideas, I keep hearing things that we've already considered at one time or another. We've had so many people working on product development for so many decades that there actually are **no** new ideas." I took that as a personal challenge, of course, and made sure the final report included plenty of surprises for him. But I also felt a pang of regret. Undoubtedly, thousands of good ideas had been developed over the course of that company's history, some going on to formal testing, some introduced to the market, but most—probably more than 90 percent—simply forgotten.

So what? Maybe they weren't good ideas. But in the world of creativity, there's no such thing as a bad idea. Ideas are like building blocks: the more and varied your blocks, the more things you can make; and you don't toss out the blocks you haven't used today—you never know

26

what you'll want or need to build tomorrow. This company (like many others) has wasted its most valuable asset by throwing out the "unused blocks." If someone had only kept a simple index-card file of each and every idea over the years, the ideation sessions would have been more efficient and maybe more productive.

If you keep a record of your ideas, then, when you need new ideas, you can start by reexamining the old ones. Some that seemed crazy a decade ago might now be viable. Others might always be crazy but serve as the spark you need to come up with more valuable concepts.

This is an important practice for **the individual** as well as for the organization. I don't keep a formal journal because I have trouble maintaining it on a daily basis (you can try this approach, though, and see if it works for you); I find it much simpler to keep an informal log or file of ideas. You can do so in a number of ways:

- Record the ideas in a notebook or journal; on sheets or scraps of paper (just label a folder "Ideas" and the scraps will tend to find their way into it); in the margins of the books and reports you read; or in electronic files (how about an idea database?).

- Use pocket message recorders: log ideas on these handy audio devices for recording "to do" items; then write down the ideas later.

2 7

- Leave yourself voice-mail. I often call my office at night and leave idea messages so I don't have to worry about forgetting them overnight.

- Use E-mail. You can create an idea address and send yourself ideas—as well as scoot others' idea-oriented E-mail into that file. Periodically, you can move the ideas into long-term storage, either on disk or on printouts of your idea file.

Of course, you can come up with your **own** approach to capturing ideas—something new and creative! The point is, countless ideas occur to you each month but a high percentage of them are lost. If you just double the number you save, your raw material for any thinking job will be enriched by 100 percent. (And don't worry about formally organizing your idea database. Random selections from it are often the most inspiring!)

3. Failure to Revisit Ideas

Whether you keep a formal record of ideas or not, you leave behind, in the wake of your daily work, many ideas and assumptions. As the path is rarely straight, you often recross your wake. But do you notice what's there or (heaven forbid!) learn from it? That's much easier said than done.

One way to revisit old ideas is to schedule yourself a little time for rambling through the debris of past projects. Every month or two, give yourself an hour to dig out old reports, peek into old working files, and leaf through old appointment books—whatever is necessary to resurface old ideas and bring into focus the context of prior decisions.

When revisiting ideas, you want to do two things:

1. Give old **ideas** a second chance.
2. Make yourself more aware of old **assumptions**.

I know it may sound confusing to divide revisiting into two separate areas—ideas and assumptions. But these areas have a distinct relationship to each other, for we can think of ideas as the **opposites** of assumptions. What do I mean? Let me explain.

Ideas represent **activity**: to generate them, we have to focus attention on something, think hard about it, get the mental gears in motion. Assumptions, on the other hand, represent **passivity**: we don't really generate assumptions so much as fall (or ease) into them, choosing **not** to think, whether we're conscious of making that choice or not. So either we think hard about something, coming up with ideas and insights, or we don't—and when we don't, we've entered the area of assumptions.

When revisiting, you often find that assumptions are more striking than ideas. You may see places where opportunities for improvement have been oddly over-looked or underdeveloped; where the validity or reli-ability of something—a process step, a planning tool, a vendor's practices—is more trusted than proved; where good, hard questions have been raised one day, only to be disregarded and shelved the next; where individu-als have simply—and dangerously—based decisions on suppositions. And if you scrutinize these places, you'll notice how assumptions tend to build a "comfort zone" around us, how they give us permission to keep avoid-ing thought and creative alternatives to the status quo.

Most organizations have powerful social mechanisms working against revisiting. Executives don't want their past decisions questioned. Team leaders and supervisors don't want to put back on the agenda an item they man-aged to get **off** it last month. And employees inevitably resist the feeling of backward motion that a reexam-ination of ideas brings with it. Add to that the danger of someone using revisiting as an excuse for playing the "blame game," and you may find that revisiting causes a level of anxiety that hinders productivity.

In such a case, you have to sell the idea of revisiting from the top down before it can be practiced successfully "in the ranks" of an organization. That's a lengthy pro-cess, as is any that requires a change of habit by top managers. But in the meantime, you can certainly begin to practice revisitation on your own. Like other creativity practices, this can be done alone or in groups. And if enough people become "closet creators" in a company, then organizational change is sure to follow.

4. Failure to Express Ideas

If you have an idea—any idea—you should express it right away. Tell it to yourself if you are alone; tell it to others if you are in a group.

That sounds like a simple, even obvious principle, but it is rarely followed. Most ideas are "nipped in the bud" by our automatic self-censorship. We never give them enough thought to figure out if they're worthwhile; nor do we share them with others. Stray ideas are treated like weeds—minor irritants to be uprooted as quickly as possible. An orderly mind has few weeds. In fact, it has little in it at all. An orderly mind is not creative. If you want creativity, you must attend to those weeds and treat each one as a potentially valuable new crop.

The weed analogy has an especially rich meaning for me. It brings to mind how my daughter, when she was four, would grill me with questions as she helped me tend our garden. She just couldn't figure out what weeds were and why they should be pulled out. "Is this a weed?" she'd ask. "What about this? Why is this a weed, but not that?" And so on, relentlessly. Finally I had to admit an essential truth about the "weeds" category: it has no botanical significance—there is no such thing as a weed from a scientific perspective. A weed is really just a plant you don't want growing in a particular place. The vegetable garden's weed may be the wildflower garden's specialty. No wonder my daughter found the category endlessly puzzling!

The same is true of ideas. We dismiss many as weeds on the assumption that they're not worth growing in our mental garden. But in doing that, we miss many potentially useful thoughts. Some mental gardens yield no crop of lasting value **except** the weeds—if the owners had the foresight to attend to them. And one very good way to attend to them is by expressing them.

Write down the stray thought, the "weed idea." Say it. Get it out of your head and into the realm of communication. That gives you the opportunity to consider it more carefully and fully—maybe to find a practical use for it as well. And it gives the thought a chance to grow and develop, possibly into more and valuable ideas.

If you get in the habit of expressing your weed ideas, you'll be surprised how easily they seed other people's imaginations. It just takes one person to get everyone in an office thinking, perhaps because they figure out that the person is having more fun than they are, and that

EXERCISE:
Generating and Capturing Ideas

1. Get a pencil and some paper, and sit down someplace comfortable. Set a time limit for yourself, at least five minutes.

2. Start writing a running monologue of your thoughts. Any thoughts. The goal is quantity, not quality. Keep writing until your time is up.

3. Calculate the number of ideas generated per minute. First, add up all the ideas you wrote; each change in topic or new angle on a topic represents one idea. Second, divide the sum by the number of minutes you took to write the ideas.

4. Record the calculation in your appointment book (where you won't lose it), and shred, rip up, or otherwise destroy the paper on which you wrote the ideas.

they can easily join the game by paying more attention to their own ideas.

If you find it difficult to "hear" and express your weed ideas, try the exercise above. Your goal is to generate as many ideas as possible and to capture them in writing. By doing this exercise regularly, trying to increase your idea count each time, you'll gain creative strength.

It's important that you complete every step each time you repeat the exercise. A word about two of the steps:

• Destroying your work. This may seem an odd instruction, particularly in light of my discussion about the importance of saving ideas. But here we're focusing on the random workings of the mind—the ultimate source of raw ideas. They could embarrass you or set off a chain of misunderstandings should a boss or a spouse come across them. They're intended for your eyes only, so don't leave them around where others might see them.

Also, you won't benefit from the exercise if you let yourself become attached to what you write. It's not art. Your ego isn't on the line. You're just pumping ions; you only do it for the mental exercise. You don't save the sweat from a physical workout, and you don't save your notes from a mental workout.

• Counting and recording the number of ideas you generated. This is important for one reason. That count has a fancy name—it's called "idea density." The higher the count, the denser your ideas—and the closer you come to the overall goal of gaining creative strength. Logging the count each time you do the exercise gives you as good a record of your progress as a weight chart does if you are on diet. When you've doubled your idea density, you've likely gotten as much as you can from the exercise.

5. Failure to Think in New Ways

You don't get out of the box by doing what you've always done. If you usually sit down and write a list of pros and cons before adopting an alternative, then you have to try a new thinking strategy to come up with anything creative. Jettison that pro/con analysis as quickly as possible. But if you never use a pro/con analysis, then by all means give it a try. I include a variety of structured creative thinking processes later in this book, but in truth, almost any approach will produce increased creativity—so long as it's **different.**

Visual thinking is usually a good choice, as most people in business don't tackle a creative task visually. So if you can't think of any other way to vary your thinking, try this approach. Draw a diagram or picture of the problem you're working on. Or think up visual analogies by asking yourself to name ten things the problem looks like. Then seek ways of generating fresh perspectives by analyzing these images (for example, why does the problem look like that thing?).

The point is that such thought patterns are novel, and so bring you quickly onto unfamiliar territory. And they draw much of their power from their novelty. So be creative about how you think about creativity (hmm, did you follow that one?). Try new and different strategies, and encourage others to do so as well.

One corollary of this last bit of advice is that it pays to discuss not just what you think but **how** you think. In any project team, office, or conference room, there are people who think in radically different ways. If you ask people how they think through a problem or issue, you may stumble upon a new approach for generating fresh ideas. You can even formalize the process by running an idea-generation session. Ask people to take turns sharing their approach to the task and leading the group through the thought process they favor. That way, everyone gets a chance to try thinking about the topic in many different ways—and everyone is forced to articulate their mental strategies, which helps make them more conscious of how they think and thus better able to take control of their thought processes.

6. Failure to Wish for More

If you're content with the current state of things, you won't feel that creative itch. Creativity is nurtured by optimistic speculation: "Wonder if we could solve that problem"; "Wish there was some way to do that." And so the failure to wish for more—for the currently unattainable—is a common way to mess up creativity.

Inventors, it seems to me, are like ordinary people in all respects but one: they always wish there were a better way. When they tie their shoes, they wish they didn't have to tie them. And so they think of using buckles, snaps, elastic, or Velcro. When they cook dinner, they wish there were some way to avoid scrubbing the sauce-pans, and so they develop Teflon-coated pans. When they return to the office and listen to their voice-mail, they wish there were some way they could avoid miss-ing important messages. And so they develop pagers. All such innovations arise from the wish to improve upon the status quo.

Yet it is far too easy for us as employees to fall into the deadening routines of our busy work lives and to slowly lose that knack of wishful thinking. It seems that life is lived at too fast a pace for any such habits to persist unless we recognize their value and make a special practice of them. And most of us don't stop to think that wishful thinking is in fact a very valuable thing.

7. Failure to Try Being Creative

I also encounter a great many people who feel they're not creative and therefore don't try to be. Well, it's this simple: you're creative if you engage in creative think-ing, and you aren't if you don't. So failure to try is the quickest way to derail your creativity. Fortunately, a little effort is the easiest way to get it back on track.

I don't think I need to belabor this point. Anyone who's gotten this far in the book is clearly willing to make a commitment to creative thinking. Just remember, it is

far more important to **do** it than to read about it. I won't
be insulted if you toss this book aside and grab a pen
and a blank sheet of paper. The sooner you start generating some creative ideas, the better!

8. Failure to Keep Trying

What, back with me so soon? Did you already fill up
that sheet of paper with brilliant ideas? Probably not.
Nothing personal, it's just that most of us don't generate
brilliant, "breakthrough" ideas when we first sit down
to do creative thinking. In fact, it's easy to generate
dozens of ideas and find that all are throwaways.

While it is easy to stimulate creative thought in yourself and others, there is absolutely no guarantee that it
will be **productive** in any practical sense. It often isn't,
at least not at first. And so we tend to abandon creative
lines of thought prematurely, discouraged by their lack
of fruitfulness. But that is a big mistake—another way
in which we all mess up creativity from time to time.

I find in my client work that no group can reliably produce valuable, profitable concepts unless they generate
ideas in the hundreds. And in my personal life, I'm often startled by the number of times I have to revisit a
topic before hitting on that breakthrough idea I need.
Creativity sometimes requires a great deal of heat to
produce any light.

If you know this before you start, you won't be discouraged by initial failure. You'll have faith in the creative process and keep working at creative thinking until you get something useful for your trouble. It might take a minute or a hundred hours to achieve the kind of breakthrough you need—but either way, you can do it.

I feel like I'm giving a pep talk here, and I guess I am; but I've seen the syndrome too many times. People think they're "stuck" when they've invested only a few minutes of thought in a problem. And organizations often accept the alternatives on the table after investing only a few meetings or work sessions in them. Yet this is the easiest mistake to avoid. All you have to do is try doubling or tripling your thinking time and see what happens. If you get good results, then increase your thinking time again: the results will get even better.

The more familiar you become with the process of creative thinking, the better you'll get at estimating the time required to complete specific "thinking tasks." You'll have more realistic expectations, and so be less apt to abandon such tasks prematurely. To start you off with a guideline, I suggest budgeting at least five hours for a major thinking task.

You must also, with **any** thinking task, give yourself time for incubation: the idea development that occurs when you "sit on a problem" for a while. Incubation is an important, not to mention amazing, part of creative thinking, for in relaxing your focus on a problem you create the conditions needed for fresh perspectives on the problem to develop.

The secret to incubating ideas is making sure to **revisit** the problem—and often. You have to keep working at it, renewing your focus and reintensifying your efforts with each return visit. This is vital because when you let the problem fall out of focus, you must not lose touch with it—you should always have a low-level aware- of it, be able to "feel" its presence in your mind. And that only happens if you put significant mental energy into the problem beforehand—if you keep trying to solve it, if you revisit and revisit again. Just toying with a problem is a superficial activity: nothing sinks into your mind, so when you set the problem aside, there's nothing to incubate!

In creativity, **effort counts**. Thomas Edison had a reason for saying "Genius is 1 percent inspiration and 99 percent perspiration": as an inventor, he knew it was the plain truth. So break the bad habit of thinking there are shortcuts to breakthrough ideas. Keep trying until you finally achieve that "Aha!" experience you've been waiting for.

9. Failure to Tolerate Creative Behavior

Creative people are a bit weird. Yes, it's true. And I say this even though I don't believe in the myth of the creative person, that is, I don't believe some of us are creative and the rest aren't. What I've found is that **when** people are being creative, their behavior seems a bit weird to others. And so tolerance of creative behavior—yours and others—is a must if you want to profit from creative thinking.

I happen to live next door to another business author, Elliott Carlisle, who first got me thinking about this problem of tolerance. He expresses the problem well in the following passage from his 1983 book *Mac*.

> [I]t's almost impossible to get any real thinking done at work. Not just because of interruptions, but almost more importantly, the whole psychological and physical environment in which managers work tends to discourage contemplation and encourage activity. The higher the level in an organization, the more critical is the role of reflection and the less important that of activity, but so often we've become conditioned on the way up through the organizational ranks. How many bosses would give a word of encouragement to a subordinate if they were to come upon him sitting at his desk, chair tipped back, foot resting on an open drawer, and staring into space with an abstract expression on

41

his face? They'd be far more likely to ask him what the hell he's doing, and if the unfortunate replied, "Thinking," he'd probably be advised to stop thinking and get back to work. (p. 12)

Yes, most supervisors communicate the "Stop thinking and get back to work" message in many ways every day. If you aren't visibly producing something tangible, then you're wasting the company's money. But ideas by their nature are invisible and intangible. So when and where can the poor employees **think**?

When I visit organizations to facilitate creativity processes, I sometimes suspect that this will be the **only** opportunity most of the attendees will get for focusing fully on creative thinking. Even if my visit is a two-day affair, I can't help wondering how the company will get along on only two days of creative thinking in an entire year of work.

If that's the case—if creative thinking is reserved for special occasions when you bring in a "creativity expert" to lead a thinking session—then your organization and its managers are making the tolerance error. And the retreat—that often-used term for those one- or two-day brainstorming sessions—is aptly named. For it is a brief retreat from an intolerant environment that does not recognize creative thinking as a valid employee activity. And the prescription for any environment from which retreat is necessary is to begin "doing" creativity at work, right in the face of such intolerance. Organizations cannot profit from employees' creative potential until their supervisors encourage and ask for creativity instead of censoring it.

⟶ ## TO RECAP:
The Nine Bad Habits

Did any of these bad habits ring a bell for you? Start working today to check them off your list of ways that you block creativity.

☐ 1. Failure to Ask Questions

☐ 2. Failure to Record Ideas

☐ 3. Failure to Revisit Ideas

☐ 4. Failure to Express Ideas

☐ 5. Failure to Think in New Ways

☐ 6. Failure to Wish for More

☐ 7. Failure to Try Being Creative

☐ 8. Failure to Keep Trying

☐ 9. Failure to Tolerate Creative Behavior

43

REFERENCES

Carlisle, Elliott. (1983). *Mac*. McGraw-Hill, 1983

Understanding the Creative Process

SOME PEOPLE LIKE FORMAL process models, with their neat 1-2-3 approach to a task. There are, in fact, lots of these models in the field of creativity and problem solving. I hate almost all of them. Why? Because they are, every one of them, linear process models. You follow their steps in strict order, one after the other, until you reach the end. At which point you are supposed to have produced a solution, as if creative ideas were machines fabricated on a mental conveyor belt.

Forget it! Creative thought does not work that way— not in the least. All these models do is hide, in a neatly numbered step, their failure to explain creative thinking. Take the common model that tells us to (1) define the problem, (2) gather information, and (3) generate a solution. Sounds logical, right? But **how** do we generate the solution? Everyone gets stuck at that point because the model has simply put creative thinking in a black box and labeled it "Step 3." But it's the key step! What we really need is a process that enables us to accomplish this step better.

And so my model (see Exhibit 3) is quite different. It involves five basic steps, but, as explained in the next section, the process for completing them is not strictly linear, just as creative thinking is not strictly linear. And it does not "frame" creative thinking in the stiff, rational structure of problem definition, information gathering, or comparative analysis of options. This a real-world model—one that works because it describes how effective creative thinkers really do their thinking. Now let's take a closer look.

THE CREATIVE THINKING PROCESS MODEL

Step 1. Recognizing Precipitating Insights

Creative thinking is precipitated by the sense of possibility we feel when something in our experience strikes us as insufficiently completed, questioned, or expressed. It may be a thing we're quite familiar with, even a task we do every day: that doesn't matter. What we perceive suddenly takes on a brighter light, a penetrating one. We glimpse underlying patterns and complexities, get an inkling of the untapped potential there. It's as if there's been a power surge in the electric lines, and in a sense, that's true: there **has** been a power surge—**in us**. Some call it inspiration. I prefer to call it **insight**, defined in my *Merriam-Webster's* as "the power or act of seeing into a situation."

EXHIBIT 3.

CREATIVE THINKING PROCESS MODEL

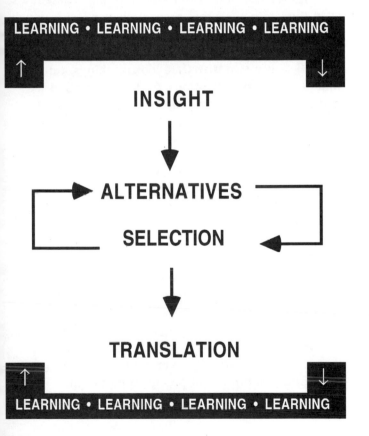

Precipitating insights are highly important because they spark the creative process, signaling that creativity is possible and appropriate in a situation. They give us direction and vision—the hope (and sometimes even the conviction) that there's a better way—which is what we need for the journey of creativity to begin. Even the simplest of insights, such as spotting a similarity between two disparate-looking things, can lead to innovations and solutions, the better way that we had hoped for. However, all precipitating insights must be given recognition and further thought if they are to lead anywhere at all.

Unfortunately, most of us don't recognize such insights. We'll get a little spark about something ("Gee, I never noticed that before") and then disregard it, neglecting to fan that spark into flames ("Oh well, it probably doesn't mean anything"). And we do little to encourage insights, when all it takes is keeping our eyes open and our minds attuned to possibilities. If we truly **look** at what's in front of us and suspend our everyday assumptions about it, the sparks can really fly.

I'm convinced that most people can greatly increase their creativity, virtually overnight, simply by recognizing the importance of precipitating insights. When you know what you are looking for, you find a lot more of it!

Step 2. Generating Alternatives

The second step in the creative process is to start generating alternatives. Alternatives are simply different ways of thinking about the topic at hand—whatever topic your precipitating insight led you to. You may immediately get into a problem/solution mode, in which case your alternatives will take the form of solutions. But that isn't always possible or desirable. Instead, you may have to consider the nature of the topic or problem itself. In which case your first alternatives are simply different views of what you are thinking about, what you want to accomplish through the creative process.

For example, suppose your topic is an everyday task that, you now realize, takes a lot of your time. You can simply say, "This task is too time-consuming," and come up with alternative solutions, different ways to do the task. Or you can look at the nature of the task and the problem: "What is it about this task that requires so much of my time? Is the real problem the task, or the conditions under which I perform the task? And why am I so concerned about time to begin with?" By asking such questions, you start generating alternative views of the situation and what you're trying to accomplish through the creative process.

Whatever form your alternatives take, the important thing is to generate lots of them. The natural growth

49

path for your precipitating insight is a branching one. Think of this step as the unfolding of a complex new plant in your mental garden, and encourage any and all branches to emerge and grow.

Step 3. Making Selections

Although we want to generate many alternative ideas and viewpoints, riotous growth will soon overwhelm us if we don't do some judicious pruning. We therefore need to select the alternatives we want to develop and cut back the rest.

As your ideas mature, this selection process will generally involve choosing between alternative solutions to a clearly defined problem. But initially the process may focus on something far more fundamental: what lines of thought to pursue in the quest for alternative solutions. Only through repeated cycles of growth and pruning will you achieve sufficient maturity of thought to propose and select well-developed options.

Step 4. Repeating Steps 2 and 3, Again and Again

Here is where the real-world model of creative thinking gets somewhat messy. One round of generating alternatives and making selections is rarely enough. Expect to return to steps 2 and 3, perhaps many times, each time seeing the problem in a slightly different light.

The selection process, with its judicious pruning, allows you to critically evaluate the ideas that have developed from your insight. And with this evaluation comes realizations. Perhaps you overlooked an interesting branch of thought that merits some attention. Or perhaps your initial view of the problem can be redefined, thus transforming the focus of the creative process.

The dynamic give-and-take between creative growth of alternatives and critical selection of them is absolutely key to creativity. Only by examining ideas with a critical eye can you see the flaws and strengths in them. And often the flaws in an idea or approach stimulate further insight and lead you to a better solution.

It should be noted that critical thinking is largely discouraged in the canon of creative thought and practice. I've attended many creative thinking sessions, some of them days long, in which participants were never permitted to voice a critical opinion about someone else's ideas. That is taking the need for supportive behavior in groups way too far. It undermines the essential dynamic between creation and evaluation, the cyclical progression toward valid solutions. In your independent thinking, and in any group creativity work you do, you need to make time for **both** generative and selective thinking; otherwise you cannot complete the creative cycles you need to "grow" your creative thoughts into anything mature and resilient enough to use in the real world of business. (Just make sure you don't criticize **people** for their ideas—only the ideas themselves!)

There is no "solution" step in this process because there is no discrete time when creative thinkers stop thinking and define the solution; that's a deceptive step to put in a process model. What really happens is that we keep cycling through alternatives and selections until it just "feels" right or makes sense to stop. Sometimes it feels right because our thought processes suddenly burst into bloom, giving us one of those wonderful "Aha!" experiences of seeing how everything falls into place. Other times, we slowly come to the realization that we're receiving diminishing returns on the time and effort we're investing—that it makes sense to stop and select the best from what we've got, and to work with that.

Either way, the creative process never really **ends**. You just decide to step out of it and harvest whatever fruit it has borne. In the long run, it is always possible to develop newer and better ideas. Creativity and innovation are, by virtue of human nature, ongoing processes, and there is always further potential to discover. So any ending to the process is really a pragmatic one, a rational or intuitive decision to switch from the world of thinking to the world of doing. For a while.

Step 5. Translating Creative Ideas

Once you have decided to switch gears from thinking to doing, you must translate your creative ideas into useful products. The expectation, at least in business, is for you to receive profitable returns on your investment in creative thinking. The products can be many and varied, depending upon your initial insight and the company's goals and needs. Here are some of the most common forms into which creative ideas are translated.

PRODUCT	DEFINITION
Solutions	Answers to tough decisions or problems
Innovations	New methods or processes
Inspirations	Powerful ideas that move or motivate people
Strategies	Ways of accomplishing challenging goals
Creations	Artistic products or performances
Inventions	New devices or objects
Problems	Re-definitions of what you are working on
Additional Insights	Understandings; new views into the hidden nature of things

Sometimes, as the last item suggests, the creative process yields nothing more than the beginning of **another** creative process. That's what it means when you say

53

"Aha, I've been looking at this all wrong!" In which case, you must repeat the entire process until you come up with another usable product. That's the way it goes. (Or, as a creative friend of mine says, "Suede goats.")

Step 6. Learning from the Process

Among the things that puzzle me about standard creativity models is that they don't have a learning loop. Many organizations discovered the value of a formal learning-loop step in process design when they adopted total quality management or process reengineering methods. The point of learning loops is to encourage future improvements rather than permit things to re-fossilize at the end of a change process. In creativity, we also need to foster continued learning and change.

What can you learn from the creativity process? First, you can and should continue to examine the subject of your creative work. Whatever the current solution, whatever you selected when you chose to stop cycling between steps 2 and 3, it is not the ultimate solution. Someday you should revisit it and try to "grow" a new and better one. So before you end any creativity process, make sure you plan for that future point. For instance, create a good archive of your ideas so you or others can revisit the thought processes later on. And make sure somebody gathers information about the new solution, whether product or process. Do people like it? What are its weak points? Does it ever fail or run into unexpected problems? How does it measure against our projections for its performance? Such questions are the stuff of future precipitating insights.

Also try to learn some lessons about the creative process itself. Did you try a new brainstorming technique? Did it help to include people from another team or department? Which thinking methods were the most useful and productive? Such questions help you become an even more effective creative thinker the next time around.

Example of the Creative Process

In case this model seems abstract to you (after all, models are just that—abstractions), here's something a bit more concrete. In this example, I've scripted the creative process for inventing an imaginary new product called Glade Blades—a name my wife, Heather, suggested that sounds so good there should be an actual product for it. Glade Blades are, as she imagined them, in-line roller skates designed for use on grass and dirt rather than pavement. The idea is that people could use them "off road," like they do dirt bikes. Great idea— but really just a precipitating insight, as it doesn't tell us how to make a product that fits this discovered need.

And so the insight leads to a natural sequence of creative thoughts concerning how to design the product. Here is how my own thoughts ran as I worked through several cycles of the creative process.

- *Precipitating Insight:* It would be fun to use roller blades "off road," like you can use mountain bikes. But roller-blade wheels are too small and hard to work on grass and dirt. Hmm. Wonder if they could be adapted somehow . . .

- *Alternatives:* Put softer rubber wheels on them. Put bigger wheels on them. Put softer, bigger wheels on them, ones that have treads like a bike wheel.

- *Selection:* Analysis reveals that none of the alternatives work well. Softer wheels alone don't do it unless they are bigger too. But bigger wheels don't fit in the wheel housing under the boot's sole. Return to generating alternatives.

- *Additional Alternative:* Center the larger wheels under the foot by raising the boot's height from the typical 2 inches or so to 6 or 8 inches above ground.

- *Selection:* The added height reduces rider stability. Who wants to skate on stilts? Back to the drawing board.

- *Additional Alternative:* Offset mounting for large wheel so that it overlaps the boot on the outside of the foot. Uses the standard boot and wheel mounting, but with an extended axle to accommodate the larger wheel on the outside. (Have to reduce the number of wheels from the standard four wheels to two or three.)

- *Selection:* Sounds good; it allows for a large wheel while keeping the foot low to the ground. But further analysis reveals that an offset wheel puts too much strain on the skater's ankle. Need to find a way to center the large wheels under the foot but not raise the foot too high. Sounds impossible, but back to working on alternatives.

- *Additional Alternative:* Put pairs of large wheels on the center line, **in front and in back** of the boot. The axles can be a little higher than the base of the boot, so the foot sits low to the ground between two large tires. Need to extend the boot in front and back with something to put the axle through. Perhaps a yoke of two aluminum pieces, bent apart to go around the boot on either side, then coming together to form a straight extension front and back.

- *Selection:* Design concept seems sound. No obvious flaws. Move to production of samples for testing. If they work, refine design and go through another creative process to translate it into something suitable for mass production.

This thought process illustrates the need for cycling between generation and selection. It took me several cycles because my first ideas proved impractical. As I explored their shortcomings, I was able to return to the generation of alternatives "sadder but wiser."

For instance, at one point I redefined my creative task, moving from the broader definition "Design a Glade Blade" to the more specific "Find a way to center the large wheels under the foot but not raise the foot too high." This view of the problem was helpful because it focused my thinking on what had emerged as the key design constraint—fitting large, off-road wheels into a skate without moving the skater's center of balance too high. When I started the creative process, I had no idea that was the key issue—I only saw the problem in that clearer light after proposing and rejecting a number of alternatives; the cyclical process at work.

Such is the nature of creative thought—and the reason why the creative process model I use, and that I advise others to use, is not a strictly linear one.

TO RECAP:
The Creative Thinking Process Model

These are the creative thinking steps we have discussed in this chapter. Remember: this is not a "regimental" process.

- ⚙ 1. Recognizing Precipitating Insights
- ⚙ 2. Generating Alternatives
- ⚙ 3. Making Selections
- ⚙ 4. Repeating Steps 2 and 3, Again and Again
- ⚙ 5. Translating Creative Ideas
- ⚙ 6. Learning from the Process

Uncreative Processes
More Classic Ways
We Close Off Creativity

CREATIVE PROCESSES—sequences of activities that are designed to generate creative thinking—can greatly enhance creative behavior in the workplace. They can help us overcome all but the most stubborn resistance to new ways of thinking and doing. Most of us are at least open enough to creativity that we can generate some good ideas if we use well-designed processes like the ones provided in this guidebook.

Conversely, uncreative processes—sequences of activities that limit creative thinking—can greatly reduce creative behavior. They often undermine enablers and can throw up such formidable barriers that even people with strong creative tendencies are constrained by them.

Maybe you're saying to yourself, "Ah, but in my organization we don't use 'uncreative' processes." If so, it's time to take another look at your organization.

UNCREATIVE PROCESSES—EVERYWHERE

Seeing the Obvious, and More

To zero in on an uncreative process, think about those staff or team meetings whose tight agenda restricts discussion topics, limits the time given to a topic, and specifies an order in which topics will be addressed. That agenda maps out a powerfully **un**creative process. It keeps people from straying off the topic, which means they are prevented from doing any speculative thinking or making unexpected connections. It blocks unanticipated thoughts—and creative thoughts are always unanticipated. It cuts off discussion so entirely that no one can return to a topic after it has "incubated" long enough for a new angle to come to mind. In short, it actively enforces an **uncreative** approach.

Consider a process we all know—brainstorming. It has a specific sequence of activities and specific rules of behavior. First, you develop a problem statement, what you are to think about. Second, you agree that everyone will free-associate to generate ideas, anything at all, and you record them on a flip chart. Third, you agree to examine these ideas with a critical eye later, after you've generated lots of them in an uncritical atmosphere. That's obviously a group process, and because it's designed to generate ideas, it's a **creative** process.

60

Now, what I find less obvious to most people is that we **constantly** design and use such group processes—things like that meeting agenda, or the customary approach to team meetings whereby each person takes the floor, in turn, to present his or her findings. There's also the staff meeting format in which the boss, equipped with standardized criteria, quizzes individual members on the performance of their section or department; and the performance review session in which the supervisor gives the employee structured feedback according to the company's standard review form. The list could go on and on. Almost everything we do together in the workplace is ritualized or formally scripted into group processes, and they structure our mental approach to work just as strongly as the rules of brainstorming do.

The problem is, these pervasive workplace processes are not designed to generate creativity; so they don't. They are **un**creative processes. And they rule our work lives! For every hour spent using a creative process like brainstorming, the average employee spends hundreds of hours following the rules of uncreative processes— without ever intending to do so. Thus workplace creativity faces an uphill battle against overwhelming odds. There's little hope of winning—of turning any workplace into a highly creative one—unless you're willing to rethink your existing uncreative processes. The rest of this guidebook will give you a positive way to do that.

WORKSHEET: GROUP MEETING PLANNER

Fill in this worksheet to make your next meeting more creative.

1. Of all the possible agenda items, which single topic
   is in greatest need of fresh, creative thinking?

   _____

   _____

2. What is the most time the group can devote to this topic?

   _____

   *(Now you have the information you need to redefine your agenda
   so you can focus the group where it will do the most good.)*

3. Who is most likely to voice creative or controversial views
   on this topic? (Include anyone who fits the description.)

   _____

   _____

4. Who is most likely to discourage or criticize creative views
   on this topic? (You're a contender for these questions too.)

   _____

   _____

   *(Now you have determined who should speak first on the topic
   [see 3] and who should speak last, if at all [see 4]. Be sure to
   structure the discussion so as to proceed in this order.)*

Combating Uncreative Processes

In the next chapter, we'll look at the building blocks of creativity, with which you can reconstruct the uncreative processes in your daily routine. Then, in Part Two, we'll look at a range of process tools that you can use to structure your own or a group's creative thinking and problem solving. As you study these, give some thought to how you might integrate a few into your daily work routine. Sure, it's nice to have an annual brainstorming session, but that won't do much to increase workplace creativity. If you want to generate a wealth of ideas, and to make progress on the Personal Creativity Matrix as well, then you need to integrate these tools into the workplace, using them to redesign routine uncreative processes. In this way, you'll replace many barriers to creativity with powerful enablers and bring out the latent creativity in you and your co-workers.

To end this topic productively, I've included a couple of extras for combating that most uncreative of processes: the staff meeting. The first is a worksheet for making your next meeting a bit more creative (see facing page). It will help you focus the group on a topic worthy of its creative potential and reduce the impact of any "heavies" who may stifle creative discussion. The second offers some guidelines and suggestions for encouraging creativity in groups and **not failing** to ask for creative ideas (see next page).

CUTTING THE UNCREATIVE OUT OF PROCESSES: Asking for Creative Ideas

One classic way we close off creativity in meetings is by failing to ask members for creative ideas. Correcting this problem largely involves paving the way for enquiry—the focus of these guidelines and suggestions.

GUIDELINES AND SUGGESTIONS

Asking for creative ideas will be far easier and much more productive if you have taken these initial steps:

- **Making the meeting safe for creativity**
- **Making time for enquiry**

To make the meeting safe for creativity, signal clearly that you're switching gears to a relaxed, supportive, nonjudgmental period of enquiry. If you normally sit at the head of the meeting table, do something to break up that authoritarian dynamic. Move to a vacant seat halfway down the table; or sit on the floor; or invite someone to lead a 10-minute brainstorming session. Try breaking the group into pairs for a quick ideation session, and join the most junior member yourself; then have each pair report their ideas to the group, and encourage an unguided discussion based on the ideas. Yes, such things add time to your meeting. That's the reason why you must also make time for enquiry.

To make time for enquiry, cut the other stuff on the agenda by half. Limit progress reports to one minute each—details can always be conveyed in writing or E-mail. Cut your opening comments, and impose a tough one- or two-minute limit on yourself. Axe all but the most important agenda items. This might seem a ruthless approach, but if you try it, you may see how much deadwood actually ends up in meetings—stuff that chokes the growth of creativity because no light can get into the process and foster that growth.

The Building Blocks of Creativity

IT IS OFTEN DESIRABLE to wear a facilitator's hat—not only when you are encouraging a group to be more creative, but also when you are boosting your creativity or that of another individual. This chapter prepares you for that role by presenting many useful actions and strategies for facilitating creative thinking. Use these as building blocks of creativity, combining them to form your own creative processes or to make existing group and individual work processes more creative.

The blocks come in a variety of shapes and sizes. There are handy little pieces, like relevant quotes that focus on creativity. You can make an overhead from one of these to use in a presentation or training session, or you can have one made into a banner at a copy shop and post it in the conference room for your next team meeting. Other, more substantial blocks include the classic process, brainstorming. You can use that block to initiate a ten- or twenty-minute period of noncritical free association as part of a group event or meeting. That's just the start. With a set of blocks such as these, you're limited only by your imagination.

| CREATIVITY QUOTES | **DEFINITIONS OF CREATIVITY** |

DEFINITIONS OF CREATIVITY

A new combination of old elements.

— James Webb Young

To break down and restructure thoughts about a topic in order to gain new insights into its nature.

— M. Wertheimer
Productive Thinking, 1945

To escape from mental stuckness.

— T. Rikards, *Creativity and Innovation Yearbook,* 1988

ON THE ROLE OF CREATIVITY IN BUSINESS

What on earth would a man do with himself if something didn't stand in his way?

— H. G. Wells

The person who walks in another's tracks leaves no footprints.

— Anonymous

Somewhere along the line, there's something more. Our job is to find it and get the public accustomed to it.

— Henry Ford

ON HOW TO BE CREATIVE

In order to compose, all you need is to remember a tune that nobody else has thought of.

— Composer Robert Schumann

Cogito, Latin for "to think," literally means "to shake together."

When you try to formalize or socialize creative activity, the only sure result is commercial constipation. . . . The good ideas are all hammered out by individuals, not spewed out by groups.

— Charles Bower

Some men go through a forest and see no firewood.

— Old English proverb

Every act of creation is first of all an act of destruction.

— Pablo Picasso

It is the child in you who is creative, not the adult. The adult in you wears a belt and suspenders and looks both ways before crossing the road. The child in you goes barefoot and plays in the street.

— Jack Foster
How to Get Ideas, 1996

The creative person wants to know about all kinds of things. . . . because he never knows when these ideas might come together to form a new idea. It may happen six minutes later or six months or six years. . . . But he has faith that it will happen.

— Carl Ally, founder of ad
agency Ally & Gargano

HUMOROUS QUOTES ABOUT CREATIVITY

Creative minds always have been known to survive any kind of bad training.

— Anna Freud

To open a business is very easy; to keep it open is very difficult.

— Chinese proverb

Dear Dr. Seuss, you shure thunk up a lot of funny books. You sure thunk up a million funny animals. Who thunk you up, Dr. Seuss?

> — Child's letter to author
> Theodor Seuss Geisel

If a man goes into business with only the idea of making money, the chances are he won't.

> — Joyce Clyde Hall, founder
> of Hallmark Cards

Name the greatest of all inventors. Accident.

> — Mark Twain

FREE ASSOCIATION AND "CREATIVE ASSOCIATION"

Idea association is one of the most basic building blocks of individual and group creativity; yet, oddly enough, there is no specific discussion of it in the traditional creativity literature. Perhaps the best-known technique for idea association is **free association**, a rudiment of the Freudian psychoanalytical method. You're likely familiar with the exercise in which a person is given a word and responds with the first thought that pops into mind: that's free association in its most basic form.

Free association is a valuable aid to creative thinking, for it helps us make connections we otherwise might not see. However, its practice as related to psychoanalysis is well beyond our purpose here. We don't need the wholesale exploration of consciousness that such idea association can lead us to. For creativity in the business sphere, we require a more focused and goal-oriented approach: we want any ideas that are **related to the topic** at hand, including many that are related to it in non-obvious ways. We also need a lot of these ideas, for a small, random sample won't help us on the problem-solving front. Thus we want to develop the art of free-associating many less-obvious but related ideas. I call this approach **creative association**.

In creative association, you free-associate so as to surface the many patterns and relationships that surround your topic and lead out from it, bringing to light related ideas along the way. This approach is facilitated by the mind's tendency to produce ideas and retrieve memories in groups, based on patterns that link them. The patterns can be formal and conscious—as when we recall that red, blue, and yellow all belong to a group called "colors." They can also be less conscious, even accidental—as when we think of "shell" and "bell" in response to the word "sell," just because all these words rhyme. An accidental or secondary association such as this one cuts a path across the more obvious (and generally more useful) main categories, connecting seemingly unrelated ideas and grouping them in new categories.

For a simple practice activity in creative association, take a word—something associated with a problem or issue at work is good—and try to find five or more association pathways from it. For example, let's take the word "late" and see how many different pathways I can find that lead us from this word to related ideas.

Opposites provide an obvious pathway for generating "early" and words associated with it, such as "ahead" and "behind." **Problems based on being late** are another obvious pathway, leading us to "service," "tardiness," "payments," and "cash flow." **Rhymes** are a good stand-by whenever you get stuck; for example, "date," "gate," and "rate"—the latter of which brings us across the second pathway, concerning late payments and cash flow issues, since late fees are essentially the rate charged customers for paying late. So we immediately have established three association pathways.

We can build a fourth pathway by **associating from one of the rhyming words**, such as "gate," which leads us to "doorway," "fence," "garden," and, strangely enough, "horses" (since horses start races from gates). For even more pathways, we can try **combining words** we have already generated, such as "gate" and "late." They suggest "missing a plane" and "getting stuck" at the gate, for example; and from there we move to words such as "ticket," "traffic jam," and "missed meetings."

To recap, these are the five pathways we discovered:

1. Opposites
2. Problems based on the key word
3. Rhymes
4. Associations from a word already generated
5. Associations from a combination of words already generated

There are many other pathways leading from "late." If you want to practice creative association, try to double or triple my number; then list all the words or ideas these paths lead you to. Here's my list:

early	payments	late fees	missing a plane
ahead	cash flow	doorway	getting stuck
behind	date	fence	ticket
service	gate	garden	traffic jam
tardiness	rate	horses	missed meetings

As you can see, you get a long listing of words that are related to your key word, if only for accidental reasons. (If you do creative association on a series of words, such as a one-sentence problem statement, you will get a list of longer ideas and phrases, though the process remains the same.) Such lists are what creativity methods like brainstorming aim to generate. Once you get good at creative association, you will find that brainstorming and the many other methods I cover in the book are helpful in creating and using lists of associated ideas.

7 1

TRADITIONAL BRAINSTORMING

Developed by Alex Osborn in the 1960s, this technique is traditionally used to help groups of six to twelve people free-associate ideas suggested by a problem statement. A facilitator or recorder commonly stands at a board or flip chart and records ideas as group members verbalize ideas in their raw form, as quickly as they occur.

Osborn drew up a set of four rules that increase people's willingness to share their ideas with the group. Usually the facilitator states or posts these rules at the start of a brainstorming session—and if necessary, politely corrects anyone who violates them. Here are the rules as I frequently state them for groups (Hiam, 1990).

1. No criticism of any ideas. Save criticisms for the evaluation stage.

2. Wild ideas are encouraged. Say whatever comes to mind.

3. Quantity, not quality. Generate as long a list as possible.

4. No proprietary ideas. Combining ideas or building on someone else's idea is encouraged.

The facilitator usually writes the problem statement for the group, making this a fairly directive method. I sometimes break that rule and ask the group to start by brainstorming what the problem is about. After ten to twenty minutes of generating creative ideas about the problem, I ask the group to switch from the Alternatives stage of the creative process to the Selection stage (see Chapter 3). We critically examine our list of ideas, working together to try to formulate several polished problem statements. Then we argue about, and/or vote on, which one to use as our focus for another round of brainstorming. (If we cannot agree on one statement, we may agree to brainstorm two or three of them in turn.)

This way, the group has a stronger hand in defining the problem. And brainstorming is used to bring creative insight to the initial stage of the creative process, often producing an "out-of-the-box" problem definition that sets us off in a new and more productive direction (see Chapter 3 for details on the Insight stage).

Once the group has developed a problem statement, I lead members into one or more brainstorming sessions in which we generate ideas related to the problem—as in traditional brainstorming. These sessions may last from five to fifty minutes, depending upon how productive the group seems to be. The facilitator's goal is to keep prodding the group for ideas until it reaches the point of diminishing returns. Experienced groups of creative people may be able to free-associate for hours on end, and so the creative departments of ad agencies use long sessions. But most employee groups run dry after fifteen or twenty minutes, so be careful not to overdo it.

EXPLORATORY
BENCHMARKING

This is the term I use for the informal, freewheeling style of research I like to do in the early stages of any project or process. Unlike traditional benchmarking (in which you carefully identify a "best-of-class" example of a product or process, study it, and model yourself after it), exploratory benchmarking is attuned to seeking novel approaches to a subject. You gather a hodgepodge of real-world examples, not all of which necessarily relate to your subject matter, and then find out just enough information about them to get the gist of what they are about or how they work. It's a quick, sweeping process.

For example, let's say you have to design the weather stripping for the doors of a new automobile. In a formal benchmarking process, you might first search out the competitor's model with the "best" weather stripping according to customer preference, then reverse-engineer it to find out what makes it the best. But in exploratory benchmarking, you would gather a wide variety of alternative designs as quickly as possible, looking as far from your industry and application as possible in order to ensure a diversity of ideas. You might sketch the designs of weather strippings used on airplane doors, boat hatches, and skylights in order to collect some "out-of-the-box" alternatives. You might even look at other sorts of seals, such as the lid of an old-fashioned Mason jar, the "skirt" used to keep water out of a kayak, the seams of space suits, and the "feet" of snails.

The product of exploratory benchmarking is an eccentric collection of designs or other ideas that may or may not be directly relevant to your subject but are certainly inspirational as you seek new approaches to the subject.

BREAK-DOWN BRAINSTORMING

I developed this method to help groups explore complex problems or projects. It uses the free-association rules of brainstorming to generate as many sub-problems as possible. Start by displaying and reading a formal statement of the problem to the group. Then point out that problem statements tend to be fairly abstract and can often be broken down into "sub-problems" or component parts. Ask the group to spend five minutes brainstorming as many sub-problems as possible, using the "No criticism" rule from traditional brainstorming. Write everything the group offers down on a board or a flip chart as accurately as possible, without editing.

The product of break-down brainstorming is a lengthy list of sub-problems. Some of these will be very helpful in formulating creative solutions to the main problem, because they will surface aspects of the problem, or suggest components of the solution, that were not visible to the group when it tackled the problem on a higher level. The method can also be used by individuals.

COMBINATION
BRAINSTORMING

I once worked on an intrapreneurship team whose task was to develop high-growth, entrepreneurial business units for a large, conservative freight transportation company. The idea made good sense, because the company was quite dependent upon a portfolio of mature, high-competition businesses, and its board recognized that it must enter some newer markets to achieve high growth. But the board also had the wisdom to know it couldn't manage a new software firm, or anything else that was too far afield from freight transportation. Whatever the new businesses were to be, they had to take advantage of some strengths the company already possessed.

This case was perfect for combination brainstorming, a method I developed in which you define the problem as "Find ideas that include x." For example, the freight transportation company was especially good at running fleets of trucks, so a worthwhile question to pursue was "Are there ideas for new businesses that include the use of a fleet of trucks?"

To brainstorm for entrepreneurial concepts that combine something creative with trucks, you can use a problem statement like the following:

Truck fleet and _____ ?

This problem statement forces creative thinking to focus on ways of combining the existing asset or strength (in this case, fleets of trucks) with other ideas to form a list of novel possibilities. Use it as you might a traditional brainstorming problem statement. Follow the basic brainstorming rules if in a group, or if alone, do whatever you need to in order to free-associate widely.

To demonstrate this method, I'll do a little combination brainstorming on the above problem statement. How about a snow-plowing business; portable computer labs in trucks that rent equipment and services by going to the customer; or a same-day distribution system for an Internet catalog sales company? What about "game trucks" loaded with the latest electronic arcade games that go to parties or set up in mall parking lots, or a re-creation of old-fashioned first class rail transport with sleeper bunks and fine dining rooms—all inside huge trucks. And so forth. You take it from here.

The advantage of this "and _____ ?" construction is that it focuses the brainstorming on ideas that meet the combination criterion—that do something new and creative **with an existing strength or asset**. The result is a more practical and "do-able" list of ideas than you would get from traditional brainstorming.

INCUBATION

We touched upon this subject earlier, in Chapter 2. If you recall, incubation is the idea development that occurs when you "sit on a problem" for a while. The extraordinary value of this building block is well expressed by Bertrand Russell:

> If I have to write upon some rather difficult topic, the best plan is think about it with very great intensity—the greatest intensity with which I am capable—for a few hours or days, and at the end of that time give orders, so to speak, that the work is to proceed underground. After some months, I return consciously to the topic and find the work has been done.

This is also a fine description of how to use incubation, of the intense focus and effort it requires in order to thoroughly drench the mental soils of your creative greenhouse in the problem.

Of course, workplace pressures conspire against such intensity. No sooner do we get started on a tough problem than a new message, report, or order distracts us. Thus anyone who wants to incubate an important problem effectively must take special care to "think about it with very great intensity," ignoring the pressures to "multi-task" instead of focus only on the problem.

One practical implication of this insight is that we should schedule our own efforts on important topics in **days** instead of hours or minutes. For example, if you devote one full day this week to studying a customer service problem, and schedule another day two weeks later for drafting a solution, then you will take full advantage of incubation and your ideas will be well developed and creative. Yet most of us would put much more than two days into such a problem without accomplishing anything creative because we'd break up that time into dozens of short efforts instead.

CYCLICAL
CREATIVITY

Cyclical creativity is a tool I use to help teams incubate ideas. It involves fewer but longer work sessions, usually off site or under "lock-down" orders to prevent interruptions. These intensive sessions are punctuated by several-day breaks, during which team members incubate ideas associated with a given problem. In the first intensive session, I recommend "overloading" the team or group on as much information about the problem as possible. In subsequent sessions, I recommend using a variety of creativity tools and processes, such as the ones in the upcoming chapters of this guidebook.

The essential feature of cyclical creativity is the use of focus/unfocus/focus cycles. Although retreat-type work sessions offer many advantages for facilitating these cycles, you can effectively integrate them into a single meeting or work session. Here's how to do it.

CYCLICAL CREATIVITY FOR SINGLE MEETINGS & SESSIONS

➦ BASIC METHOD

Alternate intensive blocks of work and meditative break periods. Devote at least 45 minutes to each work block and 30 minutes to each break period.

Take the group through at least one full focus/unfocus/focus cycle. Two or three cycles work best. Remember, each cycle entails focusing intensely on the problem and related information, relaxing focus so that ideas can incubate, and returning to focus with the ideas that developed.

➦ FOCUS PERIODS — SUGGESTED ACTIVITIES

- Use focused brainstorming techniques
- Diagram or flow-chart the problem
- Gather data on the problem or analyze data on the problem
- Write a full description or report of the work to date on the problem

The Rules: Stay on the problem. No breaks. Intensity is the key.

➦ BREAK PERIODS — STRUCTURE

It is important to structure break periods so that the problem and related ideas can "percolate." No phone calls; no chats at the coffee urn. Suggest that members take a solitary walk inside or outside the company building.

The Rules: Stay "off problem." Don't get distracted by other problems either. Disconnect is the key.

You can also use this method for incubating your own ideas. For the unfocus-cycle activities, you might turn to the following:

- Physical exercise: swimming laps, lifting weights, taking a walk, mowing a lawn

- Relaxation techniques: getting a massage, resting on a couch in a quiet room, strolling through a park

- Mentally relaxing hobbies: gardening, painting

You can also do things like wander around a shopping mall or ride a train, subway, or bus. Use your imagination to come up with other unfocus **and** focus activities: those in the method guide are just to get you started!

> **INFORMAL BRAINSTORMING**

This is a set of behavioral guidelines and "unwritten rules" that supervisors can use to stimulate creativity and free association in the daily work environment (that's what makes it informal). If you are ever in a leadership role, as a team leader, trainer, supervisor, or manager, you should study the following behavioral cues and unwritten rules and try to follow them in your interpersonal relations. You'll be surprised how many more ideas you and your associates will think of and verbalize as these cues and rules make the workplace safe for creative behavior.

81

Unwritten Rules

1. Topic-changing is OK. The requirement of formal brainstorming to focus on a single problem statement must be relaxed. This is a "creative conversation."

2. No "last word." It's not a contest. Bosses must not sum up, put down, or critique what the employee volunteers. Leave the "idea stream" un-dammed when conversations end so that further idea development is likely—and so followers will feel it is safe to share further ideas.

3. No performance demands. You don't have to come up with a "solution." Creativity can't be forced! Often a creative conversation plants seeds and nothing more.

4. No cross-use of suggestions/ideas. What's said is only for use in idea generation. It can't be referred to by the boss when wearing other hats. **Safety Zone!** signs have to go up around it.

Behavioral Cues

1. "Equalize" nonverbally by sitting in an "exposed" area. Not behind a big desk. Not higher than employee. Not in a fancier chair.

2. "Open" nonverbally by sitting in a relaxed, open posture. Don't cross legs or arms.

3. "Invite" by giving clear, verbal intention cues like "I need some zany ideas, I'm stuck on this one," and "Can you help

me with some informal brainstorming? If you toss out some ideas with me, we might stumble onto a better approach." Also, by taking the first step and voicing some silly ideas of your own, you show that your invitation is sincere.

4. "Secure" by giving clear signals that the rules apply. At first, this might mean stating them or announcing them to staff in advance—do it verbally to keep this informal. Once others know the rules, the sequence of cues in **1** through **3** above should be sufficient to secure them by signaling your intent to follow those rules.

5. "Model" by sharing your own crazy ideas, including ones that might make you look bad in front of **your** boss or peers, to show you trust that your employees/associates will "secure" you.

6. "Earn" their trust by always following the rules. Never bring their creative behavior into other areas of work. Keep their stream-of-thought suggestions "secret"—don't make jokes about what they said, put a list of "their" ideas in an E mail, or bring up something they said in a negative performance review.

7. "Reward" their participation. This means encouraging (and not interrupting!) their suggestions, and thanking them often for their help. In the longer term, it means remembering to praise them for being creative thinkers and recognizing their "ownership" of any useful ideas they helped develop (if they want ownership—check first!).

Informal brainstorming is a very powerful building block for transforming the corporate culture and daily life of a work group or organization. It helps remove many of the barriers to creativity and adds important enablers as well. If you measure employee creativity using the assessment in Chapter 1, and then train supervisors and teams in the informal brainstorming rules and cues, you should be able to measure significantly higher levels of creativity on a later repeat of the assessment.

ABSTRACTION

This is a great facilitation technique for helping people see a problem in new ways. To use abstraction, simply challenge yourself or a group to think more abstractly about your problem statement and come up with a more general statement. Let me illustrate with the following example:

- **Initial problem statement:** What should we do about the problem of high employee turnover?

- **More "abstract" versions:** How do you keep people from losing interest in something? How do you avoid losing things? How do you change someone's mind?

Once you have one or more abstract statements to work on, generate ideas relevant to them; then try to apply your ideas to the original, specific problem statement.

SEQUENCING

Another essential tool for facilitating group creativity, sequencing uses taking turns or similar rules to control the order of participation. For example, a quality improvement team might decide to take turns suggesting ideas by going around the table clockwise. Another alternative is to pass out numbered index cards from a shuffled deck and to call on participants by number (the person with "1" responds first, and so on). I recommend giving participants the right to say "pass" if they don't want to use their turn, so as to take the anxiety out of the proceedings. Sequencing is great for overcoming imbalances in group participation—it ensures that all participate and that none dominate.

PARALLELING

The idea behind this group facilitation method is to generate multiple, independent streams of thought during a group brainstorming process. Any way you can think of to encourage group members to follow and record the flow of their own thoughts qualifies as paralleling.

For example, you can hand out decks of index cards (one deck per person), adopt a topic for creative association, and then give members five minutes to write their ideas (one per card) in silence. (If you offer a reward for the most ideas, it makes the exercise fun and increases output.) At the end of the activity, gather up, shuffle, and read or list the ideas; or pin them to a board for all to examine, or lay them out on a table and let everyone argue over how to group them. Any such methods serve the purpose of sharing the ideas with the group.

It is often helpful to include brief paralleling activities in a group-oriented work process. For instance, a team working on a quality problem could start with a problem-definition brainstorming session (see the section "Traditional Brainstorming," above), then switch to a paralleling activity to generate independent ideas on how to solve the problem. Next these ideas could be shared and discussed, and then a group brainstorming period could be used to extend them.

Break-out groups and **dyads** (pairs) also are a form of paralleling. Use them to divide a group into smaller units, giving each an idea-generating assignment and a time limit (usually between fifteen minutes and one hour) and letting them go off and work independently; then have them report their results to the entire group.

An even simpler method is to give the individuals in a group or team **creativity assignments**, such as "Think of five new product concepts." These assignments can be given out before a group meeting, and you can kick off the meeting by asking people to present their ideas.

TO RECAP:
The Building Blocks of Creativity

These are the creativity building blocks we have seen in this chapter. Don't forget: they have many uses—your imagination is the limit!

- ⚙ 1. Creativity Quotes
- ⚙ 2. Free Association and Creative Association
- ⚙ 3. Traditional Brainstorming
- ⚙ 4. Exploratory Benchmarking
- ⚙ 5. Break-Down Brainstorming
- ⚙ 6. Combination Brainstorming
- ⚙ 7. Incubation
- ⚙ 8. Cyclical Creativity
- ⚙ 9. Informal Brainstorming
- ⚙ 10. Abstraction
- ⚙ 11. Sequencing
- ⚙ 12. Paralleling

REFERENCES

Foster, Jack. (1996). *How to Get Ideas.* Berrett-Koehler, p. 56.

Hiam, Alexander. (1990). *The Vest Pocket CEO: Decision-Making Tools for Executives.* Prentice Hall, p. 458.

Rikards, T. (1988). In *Creativity and Innovation Yearbook* (Vol. 1). Manchester Business School, pp. 69–77.

Russell, Bertrand. (1996). *The Conquest of Happiness.* Liveright.

Wertheimer, M. (1945). *Productive Thinking.* Harper & Row.

 PART TWO

Process Tools and Transferal

6

The Creatercize Activity

"IF IT AIN'T BROKE, BREAK IT!" That's the motto of this activity, which is a perfect creativity-boosting replacement for the many irrelevant or silly warm-up activities normally used in training sessions. Unlike most of the other activities in this guidebook, it's not aimed at generating the creative solutions you need, but at exercising your ability to generate **insights**, the kind that precipitate creative ideas—the very first stage of the creative process (see Chapter 3). Since the quality of the rest of the process depends upon the quality and quantity of your insights, this is a pretty important exercise. In fact, if you have time to use only one activity in this book right now, **make it this one!**

The most notable feature of Creatercize is that you don't start with a well-defined problem statement or goal; you start with a list of trivial problems—things that are not on your "radar screen" as needing attention because they already have some obvious solution. But is it the **best** solution? By pursuing the answer, you may get an exciting new perspective on these non-problems, even discover strategies that could streamline your company's operations or revolutionize your market. At the very least, you and others will get a better handle on the crucial first step of the creative process.

Remember, the quality of your creativity work depends upon the quality and quantity of your insights. It is thus a mistake to focus creative efforts only on **existing** problems and goals, however commonly that is done. If you have failed to define your creative agenda **creatively** enough, then you will be wasting your energy on "in-the-box" problems instead of generating novel insights and opening up new pathways for creative thought.

HOW TO USE CREATERCIZE

The Activity Steps

Creatercize has four easy-to-follow steps:

❶   Think of one or more "solved" problems.

❷   Brainstorm wild and crazy ideas for solving a "solved" problem in a non-obvious way.

❸   Identify the dumbest of your solutions and brainstorm ways to make it work.

❹   Brainstorm ways to "sell" any useful insights that are generated.

Now let's take a closer look at each step.

Think of one or more "solved" problems.

In most businesses, we have enough problems without dreaming up more just for the heck of it. But that is just what I want you to do in this step. Trust me, it **will** turn out to be beneficial in the long run.

Your target is a list of things that are **not** problems—at least, not problems you worry about, for they already have acceptable solutions at the moment. For instance, your list could include office tasks: how to make copies of a document for others to see, or how to deliver mail, run staff meetings, or hire new employees. If you work in marketing, you could cue up non-problems that apply to your customers. Let's say your product is breakfast cereals. You could list a non-problem like how to keep cereals fresh (presumably you would already be using preservatives and packaging to do so), or how to keep cereal from getting soggy in milk (people don't expect cereal to last long in milk, so this is a non-problem).

If you just want to flex your creativity muscles, then any such problem will do. If you want to maximize the chance of producing profitable insights for work, then linger on this step until you have a long list of solved problems. Then pick a few that your gut tells you may be promising and run each through the following steps.

Brainstorm wild and crazy ideas for solving a "solved" problem in a non-obvious way.

Set aside the accepted solution or solutions to the trivial or solved problem, and brainstorm a list of wild and crazy alternative solutions. Try to come up with ideas that make you embarrassed or make others laugh—the more absurd, the better. Remember, the goal of this step is to produce something that might give you an entirely new and unanticipated perspective on an old problem.

➡ **For Example**

Let's say you are considering ways of copying documents so that you can share them with others at work. The photocopy machine, E-mail, and old carbon-paper approach are obvious solutions, and they work well enough that other solutions aren't needed. Nonetheless, we want to come up with a wide variety of alternatives to them. Here's some possibilities:

- Taking Polaroid photographs of the document.

- Projecting a photographic slide of the document down a long, dark hallway; anyone with an office off the hall can could hold out a sheet of white poster board, "capture" the document's image, and read it.

- Carving the document into stone, then making "rubbings" of it with hardball wax and rice paper (the way that gravestone rubbings are usually made).

9 4

- Having an employee memorize the document and then go from office to office reciting it.

And that's just the beginning. A creative individual or group should be able to generate a hundred alternatives to the standard ways we copy documents! Here are a few more: You could use smoke signals, semaphore flag codes, African drumming, or ESP. A summary message could be printed on slips of paper and inserted in Chinese fortune cookies. You could hire a monk to create hand-lettered scrolls. Or silk-screen the document onto T-shirts and hand them out to employees. Or you could put it on a billboard next to the company parking lot for everyone to see. Or you could turn the document into a sail for a toy boat, then float it throughout the building in a water-filled trough like the ones Sushi bars use to deliver orders. Or . . . (Your turn now!)

 Identify the dumbest of your solutions and brainstorm ways to make it work.

Do any of the wild-and-crazy ideas from Step 2 inspire you? Might any of them actually **work**? In this step, you're going to find out. In fact, you're going to try to make at least one of the truly far-out ideas into something practical. So pick an idea that "obviously won't work" and start thinking about how to **make** it work. There's nearly always some way to make the wild and crazy "do-able," if you think about it for a while.

For example, you might say that a billboard is a re-
markably silly alternative to a photocopier. What a
lot of trouble and expense to get the document printed or
painted on a thirty-foot-long board! Hardly an efficient alternative. But can we make it work somehow? Is
there any real-world scenario in which this idea might
be a good alternative to photocopying a document?

Well, if you really think about it, some kinds of messages are well suited to this medium. If a company had
a billboard in the employee parking lot, they would
surely find some uses for it. General announcements and
reminders might be put on it. And what a great way for
management to say "Thanks!" when employees achieve
a production or quality goal! Perhaps the president
would want to convey a weekly message on the board.
There are probably lots of ways to use this medium as a
complement to other communication methods. And I
never would have thought about it if I hadn't used the
Creatercize activity to solve a trivial problem.

➡ **Repeat or Expand This Step?**

You may find that several of your "silly" ideas have a
kernel of something useful and practical in them. If so,
by all means please break this step's rules and brainstorm ways of applying multiple alternatives. (Never
let a formal creativity process stifle your creativity!)

For instance, I can imagine times when you might prefer to hire a calligrapher to hand-letter copies of a message, such as a congratulatory letter to a successful process reengineering team. So the "monk" idea from Step 2 is practical as well. Same with the idea of putting your message on T-shirts and handing them out. I might prefer this approach over sending out a memo if I wanted to tell employees about an inspiring new goal for the organization, for example.

 Brainstorm ways to "sell" any useful insights that are generated.

If you have some success with Step 3, then you will already have application-oriented insights as you enter this final step. The point of this step is simply to ensure you "capture" and follow up on any good ideas. Follow-up is particularly difficult in this activity because you aren't focusing on current priorities, but looking to "resolve" trivial problems. So whatever you come up with, it is by definition a solution nobody was looking for.

You now have to convince relevant decision-makers that your idea deserves their attention. I recommend that you begin by brainstorming how to "sell" your new ideas. Don't just write a memo to the person in charge of corporate communications, suggesting it would be fun to erect a billboard in the parking lot. If no one's currently looking for new ways to get messages to employees, then the memo will end up in the proverbial circular file faster than you can say "Wait a minute."

➤ For Example

How can you sell senior managers on the idea of erecting a billboard for employee communications? You'll need to catch their attention and then convince them that billboards are a potentially powerful medium. Perhaps you could rent a billboard along their commute route and put a message to them on it. If your budget is limited, you could simulate the effect by writing them a brief note on a sheet of poster board and putting it up in their office while they are out. Or, if you know how to play around with photographs on one of those computer darkroom programs, you could combine a picture of a billboard with a picture of the company parking lot to show them what it would look like—complete with the text of your choice.

The Magic Toolbox

MANY CREATIVITY CONSULTANTS use analogies to "force" creative thinking. Exercises such as "Compare your problem to a toaster" are common. I have mixed feelings about them because, to be honest, I often cannot find meaningful similarities between real-world problems and toasters. Nor can many groups. Yet sometimes an absurd analogy will inspire creative thinking and prove highly worthwhile. So that leaves us with a dilemma: how to take advantage of the benefits of analogies but avoid artificial, difficult "force fits."

This method is one solution I stumbled across in my own creativity work. It uses a toolbox full of tools as a metaphor. I like it because, for some reason I haven't really figured out, tools are rich, relevant metaphors for the kinds of things we work on in business. Maybe it's because tools have a basic relationship to business, at least for carpenters. But whatever the reason, I think you will find it easy to draw meaningful comparisons between your topic of concern and commonplace hand tools. Give it a try!

HOW TO USE THE MAGIC TOOLBOX

The Activity Steps

The Magic Toolbox has three basic steps:

❶ Write a focus statement defining a general focus or a specific problem.

❷ Think of uses for a wide variety of "magic" tools.

❸ Explore the results for inspiration.

Here are the details for following each step.

 Write a focus statement defining a general focus or a specific problem.

Whether your statement is general or specific will depend on how clearly you can see the situation (general focus for Step 1 of the creative process, specific problem for Step 2; see Chapter 3). The method does not demand a well-defined problem, and in fact can be used to surface problems. But if you do have a definite problem, you can produce focused solutions via the method. Thus, any of the following focus statements are fine, and could be posted or read at the start of the activity. Note that they range from very general to quite specific.

- What should the human resources function focus on right now?

- What sort of human resources plan do we need in order to be prepared for a downsizing?

- How can we increase employee motivation after a downsizing?

 Think of uses for a wide variety of "magic" tools.

This is where you get to use your imagination and to help others do so if you're facilitating a group. To start, ask yourself or your group to consider this statement:

If I/we had a magic drill, we'd use it to _____.

Come up with a way to use this "magic drill" to work on the topic of your focus statement. For example, a group might take the problem, "How can we increase employee motivation after downsizing?" and come up with answers like "We'd use a magic drill to make holes in everyone out of which the bad feelings would leak." Collect one or more (many more if possible) of these ideas and write them down for later analysis.

Keep going until you and/or your group run out of tools and uses for them. Here are some of the other things in a typical toolbox that you can use, along with examples of how a group might use them to turn employee motivation around after a downsizing.

➡ **Tools and Examples**

- *Saw:* Cut the new, downsized company free from its past for a fresh start. Cut boards and use them to build miniature forts to protect the remaining employees from another round of downsizing.

- *Hammer:* Hammer nails into the coffins of those who have left. Bang out the dents from our recent collision with trouble.

- *Duct tape:* Wrap it around us to bring us back together again. Tape managers' mouths shut so they can't announce another downsizing for a while.

- *Screw driver:* Tighten the screws that came loose from the vibrations when the organization was forced to operate in overdrive.

- *Tape measure:* Check that employees' feelings about the company still "measure up."

- *Level:* Even out the work loads to make sure extra work from the downsizing is distributed fairly.

- *Pry bar:* Tear down and discard the walls that were built up during the downsizing, so that we can rebuild communication lines and trust.

- *Glue:* Fix the cracks left in employees' feelings.

Explore the results for inspiration.

What you get in Step 2 are fantasy solutions, none of which would work in the "real world." That's OK, because they may lead to insights that **do** apply to the real world. Look at your answers (or the group's) to see what kinds of **feelings** and **images** are arising. Also look for **actions** and **goals** that make sense and could be accomplished with real-world tools.

In the above example, the group uses its magic tools to protect employees, to pull them back together, to allow bad feelings to leak out or be cut free, to measure how people feel, and to fix problems caused by the downsizing. These are extremely relevant actions and goals, and you can certainly come up with ways to do the same things using the real-world tools available to you.

While you cannot use magic tape to "bring everyone together," an event of some kind might do the trick. Nor can you use a magic measuring tape to find out how people feel, but it's a good idea to survey them in order to measure attitudes like anxiety, fear, and stress. If these negative feelings are still high, then perhaps you do need to "tape managers' mouths shut so they can't announce another downsizing." Maybe management would be willing to announce a stability period of one year, during which they promise not to make more cuts. Similarly, a magic level doesn't exist, but the notion of balancing work levels is a sound one and ought to be part of the recovery from downsizing.

The results of this simple analogy exercise often inspire many practical ideas like these. See, I told you: the toolbox analogy really does work!

➡ **Variants of the Magic Toolbox**

You can also brainstorm uses for magic kitchen tools or cleaning tools. These categories also seem to generate many rich and useful analogies. I call these "The Magic Kitchen" and "The Magic Closet" for obvious reasons.

Three-Step Word Association

WHEN PRESSED TO DEFINE CREATIVITY, I usually say that it's new and useful combinations of thoughts. (When not pressed, I avoid defining it, since getting too scientific about creativity is a violation of its spirit). In this process tool, which is suitable for individuals or groups, you use word associations to generate unexplored combinations of words and ideas. Then you try to make these combinations useful and relevant. And, with a little luck or enough persistence, you end up with new and useful idea combinations. Here's how to do it.

HOW TO USE THREE-STEP WORD ASSOCIATION

The Activity Steps

There are four steps in all. The first three focus on word association; the fourth involves generating new ideas.

❶ Brainstorm a list of relevant words with clear associations to your subject.

❷ For each relevant word, brainstorm a list of irrelevant words.

❸ Transform each irrelevant word into one or more relevant words.

❹ Play with the new list of relevant words to see if any lead to breakthrough ideas.

We'll take a closer look at each of these steps, but first we need to deal with two preliminary considerations, both of which are related to the activity's structure.

➥ Recording the Associated Words

You'll need some kind of format for recording and stimulating ideas. A three-column table works well, with a generous amount of space for the middle column. If using a wall board of some kind (best for a group), reserve a full-height column on the left-hand side, about two feet wide, and add a second column of double the width. Leave the rest of the board blank so that your third column can expand as needed. If you're working on your own, use a large sheet of paper if possible; in a pinch, you can use standard-size paper and add new sheets on, using staples or tape, as your ideas expand. Another possibility is to do your independent thinking on a wall board or flip chart (my preference).

Leave room at the top of the wall board or paper for your starting-point statement (more on that later), and label the first column "Relevant Words," the second "Irrelevant Words," and the third "Transformations."

➡ Process Rules

These are not needed, but they can be helpful if you're working with large, shy, or overly vocal groups, or if you get stuck when working on your own. In other words, don't add structure for its own sake—use it for trouble-shooting. Start with the simplest approach to group association, which is to have someone be the recorder and everyone shout out their ideas. If this is too confusing or not productive enough, try a structured approach such as speaking in turn or alternating periods of independent work and group sharing (see Chapter 5 for more ideas). Now let's take a look at each activity step.

 ### Brainstorm a list of relevant words with clear associations to your subject.

Apply the rules of formal brainstorming or simply free-associate to come up with a list of relevant words. Don't worry too much about how you define the subject at this point, as the activity is easy to repeat, whether you're working independently or in groups. In case you get stuck before you get started, here are some suggestions.

➡ Defining the Starting Point for Free Association

Let's say that you need a name for a new warehouse store specializing in bedding, bedroom furnishing, and other sleep-related products. You might simply define the starting point as something obvious like "What we

107

call our new store." But if this doesn't seem to work (to lead to many relevant words quickly), then try something with more "sticky ends," which is what I call **words that attract associations**. For instance, you could say, "What words are associated with a store that carries bedroom furnishings and linens?" This is a better starting point partly because it has more words in it—particularly nouns, which are easy to associate from ("store," "bedroom," "furnishings," and "linens" all evoke their own chains of associations). It is better also because it evokes a rich visual image, of a store filled with lots of merchandise that you can "see" and name. (Lesson: It is always easier to free-associate from goal or problem statements that evoke visual images than from ones without much imagery.)

➡ Free-Associating

Once you have a starting point, begin listing obvious associations, word by word, in the first column. No need for any special creativity here. Say you want to develop ideas for how to solve a union-management dispute; you would just list words like "strike," "anger," "tenure," "temps," "raises"—whatever words are in your mind at the moment. Not hard at all!

Generate at least a dozen words—much more if the subject permits. In either case, stop after ten minutes or so, as you want to save energy for the rest of the activity.

108

For each relevant word, brainstorm a list of irrelevant words.

Now go back to the first relevant word you listed and use it as a starting point for a list of irrelevant associations: words that are suggested by alternative meanings of the relevant word, or that have some nonsensical but clear relationship to it. Try to come up with at least three irrelevant words for each relevant word. Enter the words into the middle column. Then repeat the process, generating more or fewer irrelevant words based on the ease with which they occur to you.

If this step sounds more difficult than the last, that's because in some ways it is; irrelevant words tend to be less obvious than relevant ones. But it's still pretty easy, especially once you get the hang of it. To help you along, I'll return to the problem of generating ideas about a labor-management conflict.

Let's say your first relevant word is "strike." You might think of a strike in baseball, and associated words like "baseball," "pitcher," "umpire," and "home plate." Or you might think of the word as a verb: to strike something. This suggests words such as "hit," "pound," and "hammer." You might recall the expression "to strike a tune," and think of words like "note" and "melody." There's also the expression "to strike a pose." Or you might think of "striking their colors," as when in battle

109

those on the losing side (or their conquerors) take down their flag. Then your irrelevant words would include "flag," "colors," "battle," "ship," and the like. (Lesson: Associate by thinking of a word's alternative uses.)

Another way to come up with irrelevant words is to vary the word slightly so as to change it into another word. For instance, if you happen to know something about birds, you might turn "strike" into "shrike" and think of words like "bird" and "feather." Or you might turn it into "spike" or "mike" (as in "microphone"), as that rhymes with "strike." As these examples show, it's not hard to associate irrelevant words. You may find you run out of room for them in your column once you become familiar with the task—in which case, go over the line into the third column and draw a new line later on—no point in losing ideas just to keep things neat!

One thing I do want you to do in the neatness department, however, is keep track of the relationship between irrelevant and relevant words. If your page gets too full, words will begin to run together, so consider drawing a box around each set of irrelevant words, then drawing a line to the relevant word from which each set arose. Why keep track? Because you may wish to re-create a chain of thought, perhaps because you wandered from it and got lost, or maybe just out of curiosity about how you generated good ideas.

110

3 Transform each irrelevant word into one or more relevant words.

Your excursion into irrelevant word associations gives you a lengthy list, but not a very useful one. In fact, it's probably quite silly. That's the point, because you're now going to try to combine some of these irrelevancies with one or more **relevant** words to form useful phrases and ideas. Why? Because this is a relatively easy way to achieve that creative goal of finding new and useful combinations of ideas.

Try transforming the irrelevant words I listed above for "strike" into something useful in the context of a labor-management dispute. Take "umpire," for instance. Can you generate any relevant ideas that use this word? Perhaps it suggests that an umpire-like person might be useful in certain types of labor-management disputes— a "third-party arbitrator" who can keep "the game" running smoothly until negotiations are completed.

Please note that you need not force every irrelevant word into a relevant idea. Some creativity experts insist that any novel or nonsensical combination of ideas can lead to a breakthrough insight, but I don't find that a practical philosophy. In reality, you will come upon some irrelevant words that are quite difficult to transform. That's OK. Just leave them. A few may incubate and lead to something later, but most are probably dead

111

ends. In my experience, I've found it takes many dead ends to come up with even one truly valuable idea. This process generates irrelevant words quickly, so you can easily afford to "waste" words if they don't suggest a useful idea right away.

➭ For Example

I worked out one example above, but it will be helpful to supplement this with a graphic of what your work should look like. Exhibit 4 illustrates several chains of thought for the earlier problem of what to call a new warehouse store specializing in bedroom products. The results include my favorite, "The Slumber Yard"—a pretty good idea and certainly a novel one!

➭ The Free-Association Wheel

This alternative to the table format is made up of three concentric circles. Here's how to use it:

1. Draw a small circle in the center of your board or paper and enter the goal or problem statement (your starting point).

2. Around that, draw a larger circle, in which to enter relevant words/images.

3. Around that, draw a much larger circle, in which to enter irrelevant associations for each relevant word/image.

EXHIBIT 4. Sample Table

★ THREE-STEP WORD ASSOCIATION ★		
GOAL: Find a new name for a warehouse store specializing in bedding, bedroom furnishings, and other sleep-related products		
RELEVANT	**IRRELEVANT**	**TRANSFORMATIONS**
sleep		
bed		
pillow → →	willow, tree, free, fluff, feather,	
PJs	Eider down → → → → →	**Down Home**
rest		
slumber →	slumber party, lumber,	
feathers	lumber yard → → → → →	**The Slumber Yard**
sheet → →	sleet, sheet of paper, sheet	
pillow case	music → → → → → →	**Sheet Music**
dream → →	sleep, scream, "to sleep,	
nightmare	perchance to dream" → →	**Perchance to Dream**
alarm		
clock → →	→ → → → → → → →	**Alarms & Diversions**
curtain		
night stand		
dresser →	storage, clothes, lingerie →	**Bedroom Personals**

4. Use the area outside the circles to jot down transformations (new relevant words) as they occur to you.

I like this format because it accommodates rapidly expanding chains of thought. Each new circle adds a much larger area for writing than the one inside it. And it's easy to keep track of each chain of thought by adding lines that radiate outward, dividing the circle into sections as needed.

 Play with the new list of relevant words to see if any lead to breakthrough ideas.

Now that you have a new list of relevant words and ideas, you have something to play with that may indeed generate breakthrough insights. Sometimes the breakthrough idea and the relevant idea will simply be one and the same; "The Slumber Yard," for instance, may be precisely what you want ("Aha!"). At other times, you may have to "play" with relevant ideas, giving them more thought. "Third-party arbitrator" is the kind of relevant idea that may need further development before it can lead you to a breakthrough. You might try to imagine who this arbitrator would be (a hired expert?) or what kind of power he or she would have (interim power to impose quick decisions to keep "the game" proceeding smoothly?). Of course, you may come to a dead end; but then again, you may come to the juncture of a creative throughway!

114

Category Expansion

WE OFTEN HEAR PEOPLE SAY, "Let's get out of the box," but this is difficult advice to follow when you don't know what the parameters of the box might be. Sure, our thinking must be constrained in some manner, but how? Category Expansion offers you a systematic way to identify the parameters of your current mental box and then seek new and different boxes, or at least different perspectives on the current box. It is especially useful in Step 1 of the creative process (see Chapter 3 for details).

HOW TO USE CATEGORY EXPANSION

The Activity Steps

Here are the five steps of this activity:

❶ Choose your focus: write a simple problem definition or general purpose statement.

❷ Define existing categories of ideas and solutions that are related to your focus.

❸ Look for ways to fit smaller categories into larger, higher-level categories.

❹ Look for new category members.

❺ Explore solutions from new categories and items.

Now for the explanation of each step.

 Choose your focus: write a simple problem definition or general purpose statement.

For Step 1, you don't need a narrowly defined problem statement; any general topic statement will do, as you will soon be exploring its parameters in ways that will lead to redefinition anyway. Here are some examples:

- How do we raise money to help us overcome short-term cash flow problems and fund our expansion?

- What should we do about the rising accident rate on the factory floor?

- How can we reverse our product's drop in sales?

- Are there new and useful ways to think about new product development?

- Are there alternatives to our standard approach to employee rewards and motivation?

Problem definitions are usually part of the "box" so don't belabor this step—just pick a starting point and go to the next step.

Define existing categories of ideas and solutions that are related to your focus.

Now make a list of words and phrases associated with common ideas about, and solutions for, your problem or goal. These are the existing answers for which you want to find creative alternatives.

Once you have listed everything that easily comes to mind, stop and think about how to **categorize** the items. Is every item in the same category? If so, give the category a name. Are there two or three categories? Name them and rewrite your list as several lists, each with an appropriate category heading.

➡ **For Example**

Let's say you are exploring ways to prevent accidents in logging crews (logging is a profession with high injury and death rates), and that, in Step 1, you came up with "Are there any new ways to think about accidents?" Now you might make a list of related ideas such as:

Chain-saw injuries	Access to medical facilities
Fatigue	First Aid supplies/training?
Lack of training?	Protective goggles/ear plugs
Trees falling on workers	(Do workers wear them?)
Accidents with vehicles	Problems with hearing
Supervision (Enough of it?)	instructions/warnings

117

This is not a formal list of the causes of accidents, nor of prevention methods, though many causes and methods appear in it. Basically it is the "core dump" of topics already in one's memory—the "top-of-mind" stuff that is easy to access when thinking about a topic.

Whenever you work on a problem, you begin with a similar list of accessible ideas. For instance, if you wanted to improve the safety record of a logging company, you might start by addressing the question-marked items above. Yet, as logging has been a highly hazardous profession for years, such in-the-box thinking may not work; that's where this creative process tool comes in.

To finish this step of Category Expansion, you need to categorize everything in your list. Luckily there is no right way to do so—any assortment of categories will do. For instance, you might categorize the list above into these three categories:

- Processes
- Equipment
- People

Access to medical supplies and treatment fit the "Processes" category. Safety gear, work gear (like chain saws), vehicles, and other gear can be put in the "Equipment" category. Injuries, communication problems, and supervision and training fit the "People" category.

➡ **Trouble with Categories?**

If for some reason you get "stuck" and can't seem to find categories for your list items, try using what Japanese quality experts use—the five classic categories of the cause-and-effect diagram: "Material," "Machine," "Measurement," "Man," and "Method." Although they may not fit your needs exactly, they will steer you in the right direction, getting you started on customizing your own categories.

③ Look for ways to fit smaller categories into larger, higher-level categories.

If you have defined only one category, then obviously you have a high-level one to start with—but you still may be able to put it in a larger category. If you came up with several categories in Step 2 (as people often do), you can certainly find one or more higher-level categories by asking what things your categories have in common. Ask yourself what the relationships between the categories might be. Are they naturally part of any larger category?

➡ **For Example**

Let's continue with the logging-safety problem. Step 2 resulted in three categories: "Processes," "Equipment," and "People." What do all of them have in common? You might say they all have to do with things that go on at the logging site; therefore they can be put into the broad category "Forest Operations." Once you state a larger category such as this, it's often easy to see the possibility of even larger categories. Case in point: the "Forest Operations" category suggests the existence of other company operations and functions, all nested within the "Company Operations" category—which itself can be put in the category "Industry Operations." Ideas like these flow quite easily when you ask yourself or a group to think of categories.

 Look for new category members.

When we define any new category, it's natural for us to want to add new members. That's because our memories tend to organize things by category, so categories give us access to memories. Suppose I ask you to name things that belong in the "Birthdays" category; you can easily say, "Presents, cake, ice cream, cards, ribbons, decorations, parties," and the like. It isn't hard to generate a fairly exhaustive list of everything that belongs in the category. Anything missing tends to pop into mind when you review the list or someone else does (you may have noticed that my "Birthdays" list doesn't directly mention birthday candles or the "Happy Birthday" song).

Take advantage of your natural ability to expand upon category lists by now adding more items to the category groupings you made in earlier steps. Some of these items will be categories in themselves, since Step 3 produced nested categories; so you're adding not only to within-category lists but also to the number of categories.

➡ For Example

Let's return to logging safety. In working on Step 4, you may realize there should be a "Support Operations" category at the same level of hierarchy as the "Forest Operations" category (a result of Step 3). Presumably, there are support staff and facilities near any logging site. Yet if you had not gone through the exercise of ex-panding your list, you may not have thought to include them in potential solutions to the safety problem. This new category might not necessarily inspire "the solu-tion," but at least you're out of your mental box and thinking about the problem from a fresh perspective!

 5 **Explore solutions from new categories and items.**

Our mental boxes generally limit us to solutions based on familiar categories. Now that you've expanded the number of categories and added new items to categories, you have a simple way to get out of the old box. Just use the new items and categories to "free up" your thinking. To start exploring, ask yourself (or your group) questions like "Are there any alternative approaches based on

121

unfamiliar categories?" You can also review the "in-the-box" approaches to the problem, checking to see which categories they belong in. You may find they're even more narrow than your initial list suggests!

➡ For Example

Let's return a final time to the logging-safety problem. Suppose it turns out that most safety efforts fall into the "Forest Operations" category, including gear, work rules, First Aid, and emergency phones; but despite such strategies, your workers still get injured. So you now turn to other categories. "Industry Operations" might lead you to consider the high pressure to produce in the logging industry, which forces competitors to push their workers hard. Is there some way to create an industry-wide safety certification that's awarded to companies who achieve low injury rates? If the high death and dismemberment rates of logging were publicized, this certification could become meaningful to industry consumers, countering the current emphasis on productivity at any cost. **That's** an idea worth following up!

HOW TO "DRAW" CATEGORY EXPANSION

It helps to work visually with your categories, to map out your progress on them. I use a simple visual method: circles and lists (see Exhibit 5). All it takes is a big

EXHIBIT 5. Category Map

writing area. And I prefer an erasable medium so I can reorganize as I go along. A big erasable wall board is great, but a pencil and paper (or paper and sticky notes) work fine for individual efforts.

Exhibit 5 illustrates how I draw my mental map of categories as I use Category Expansion. It shows a well-developed category map for the problem of how to find creative ways to reward employees for exceptional work. For a number of years, the company in question had run an annual Employee Appreciation Day, and so the initial "core dump" of items associated with employee rewards fell into this category. In later steps, new categories and items were added.

Surfacing Assumptions

WHEN ARCHAEOLOGISTS translated 4500-year-old carvings on an Egyptian pyramid, they were surprised to discover medical advice that included the following item: "If a patient with a neck injury has loss of feeling in the arms and legs, it is because of a break in the spinal cord. . . . This condition cannot be treated" (*New York Times*, Sept. 30, 1997, p. C1). Today, we still view spinal cord injuries as essentially untreatable for the simple reason that severed nerve tissues in the spinal cord do not regrow. It's as if you had cut off the limb of a tree—while the tree survives, the limb dies away and is lost. But trees can grow new limbs. Why not people and other mammals?

By asking this "Why not?" question, I'm surfacing an assumption—a 4500-year-old assumption. I'm no scientist, but some people who are have begun exploring this same creative path. Research has shown that olfactory nerve cells—the ones responsible for smell—do regrow after injuries. Now researchers are experimenting with injecting these cells into the injured spinal cords of lab mice to see what happens. To date, they have demon-

125

strated at least partial regrowth of spinal nerve tissue. So it may soon be time to retire a very old assumption!

Most workplace assumptions do not go back to ancient Egypt, but they might as well be carved inside a pyramid, for they can be just as hard to find and to change. There are many hidden assumptions in every decision we make, whether we decide to act or not to act. And one of the most powerful ways to see new opportunities is to explore these assumptions. This process tool offers three activities that will help you (or a group) do so.

1. Surfacing Assumptions
2. Surfacing Obvious/Trivial Assumptions
3. Reversing a Key Assumption

We'll look at each one in turn.

SURFACING ASSUMPTIONS

It can take considerable creative insight to even recognize an assumption, which is why an activity like this one is so useful. Its two question formats (see next page) are designed to structure assumption brainstorming and to "trigger" idea generation. For the best results, repeat them several times with minor variations. Be sure to include **every** assumption that occurs to you, even if the list reaches into the dozens (I use eight items in the formats because I find that groups get stuck at four or five.

SURFACING ASSUMPTIONS: QUESTION FORMATS

➤ SET 1: Positive Assumptions

We plan to _____

in order to accomplish _____

_____

What are our assumptions? That:

1.	5.
2.	6.
3.	7.
4.	8.

➤ SET 2: Negative Assumptions

We can't _____

because _____

_____

What are our assumptions? That:

1.	5.
2.	6.
3.	7.
4.	8.

127

If you push groups to come up with eight, then the going is easy from there on out).

➡ For Example

A successful regional retailer fills in the Set 1 form as follows: "We plan to open stores in additional cities and states in order to maintain our fast growth rate." Great idea. Or is it? Almost every retailer has considered this simple expansion strategy, but it only makes sense if the assumptions the retailer listed are valid. Here's the list:

- Our store concept is broad (isn't regional in appeal).
- Demand for our store concept will continue to be high.
- The best way to grow fast is to open new stores.
- Fast growth is necessary and healthy for us.
- We can handle more stores if we open them.
- We can open more without taking unacceptable risks.
- We can find good store locations for rent.
- If we grow our sales by opening stores, our profits will grow proportionately.
- Competitors won't open up similar stores elsewhere first, preempting our strategy.
- We can find competent employees for our new locations at reasonable cost.
- It isn't feasible to grow fast by expanding in our current locations/markets.

128

By exploring these assumptions, the managers of this business are likely to generate a variety of creative insights and to arrive at some interesting alternatives to their current plan. For instance, they might reconsider the assumption that it isn't feasible to expand their existing stores, and think about converting a few into superstores. They could decide to experiment with their store layouts and product selection; or they might work on cutting costs and adding higher-value, higher-priced items so as to grow profits rather than revenues.

Some of these alternatives could have escaped serious consideration because of **limiting assumptions**. Let's say the managers questioned the last assumption on their list, filled in Set 2 with "We can't double or triple revenues in an existing store because we already gross around $750,000 per year," and listed "The industry maximum is $750,000" as one assumption. By exploring this negative assumption and others, they may find their choices are not as limited as they first believed.

Their Set 1 list may include **dangerous assumptions** too, ones in need of serious thought before any plan is implemented. If the managers haven't thought hard about the future appeal of their store concept, they should do that now. If it's a fad, or if it could be knocked off by discounters, then they need to focus on concept innovation before they worry about expanding to new sites.

SURFACING OBVIOUS/TRIVIAL ASSUMPTIONS

Some assumptions seem obvious and trivial. You may feel they aren't worth questioning because they don't significantly affect your decision making—or even if they do, you may feel you can't do anything about them. Please, please, include them anyway. They may lead you to other, important assumptions. You may even see these so-called trivial assumptions in a new light later on, finding creative ways to make them significant. So don't hold back: include anything of possible relevance.

➡ **For Example**

If you assume that the sun will keep coming up, state that. I know you can't change it, but it still might prove relevant. Suppose you were in the business of selling sunglasses. Your next year's marketing plan would certainly depend upon this assumption—perhaps in more subtle, relevant ways than expected. You might look at the assumption "The sun will come up" and think of related assumptions like "The sun will be bright," "It won't be cloudy," and "People will go out in the sun." Each of these is more likely to be variable and thus to affect short-term demand for sunglasses. What if many people start to spend more time indoors, or go outside in the morning and evening instead of at high noon? What about people whose sun exposure is limited to the daily commute and the occasional morning or evening jog? At these times, sunglasses may be inadequate for the combination of shadows and blinding, low-angle sunlight.

If you ponder the above, you may come to the same conclusion I did: that most lens designs for sunglasses are based on some false assumptions about usage, and that at the very least they could be modified to suit early- and late-day lighting conditions. Perhaps lenses with dark peripheries and lighter centers would do it. Or better versions of light-sensitive lenses. Or lenses that, with a quick touch, can be rotated one way for light protection and the other way for seeing into shadows (modeled on polarizing light filters for cameras). As this simple example shows, surfacing and exploring the obvious and trivial can lead to many creative insights!

REVERSING A KEY ASSUMPTION

I once reviewed a marketing plan for a T-shirt company whose success was focused in one major city. Company planners had gathered statistics on the average number of fashion (silk-screened) T-shirts owned by the typical resident of various other cities, and had found their city residents owned more than the average. This, combined with a slowing sales-growth rate, convinced the planners that the local market was saturated and that they needed to open shop in four new cities in order to maintain their desired rate of growth.

Their plan included details of how to produce and market products in four new cities with lower per capita ownership of T-shirts. Would it work? Was it the best approach? To find out, I surfaced lots of assumptions, then asked myself which were the most important. I felt the assumption of **market saturation** was the key, since it was what led them to look beyond their current market in the first place. And so I tried **reversing** this assumption in order to learn more about it.

When you reverse an assumption, you try to find an opposite version of it that might be true. This is a little tricky, since there may be multiple opposites and partial opposites to consider. If so, just write them all out. There are no wrong or right answers as long as you wear your creative hat when reversing an assumption. Here are some of the reversals I considered:

Assumption: The market for T-shirts is saturated when per capita ownership rises above the national average. Therefore consumers will buy fewer shirts when they own more.

Reversals?
- The market is not saturated in spite of the statistics.
- The saturation assumption does not apply to T-shirts.
- People who own more T-shirts will buy more, not less.

You may very well be thinking, "Those reverse assumptions look like total nonsense!" And in fact they should. Reversals of common assumptions turn conventional wisdom on its head. They violate common sense. And often, all you learn is that conventional wisdom was right. But sometimes (more often than you might expect), you discover that conventional wisdom doesn't apply. You discover some new way of looking at the situation. And then it's easy to come up with a creative approach that wins out over anything based on the old assumption.

As in this case. Because if you think hard about the T-shirt market, you may well decide that the reverse assumptions are more valid than the conventional, starting assumption. Really. The idea of a saturation point is based on the assumption that the consumer only needs so much of a particular product. And that is generally true. How many refrigerators does a household need? Not many. Once you've sold most households their first refrigerator, the market is saturated. Future sales will be slower, limited by the replacement rate for the product. That is certainly true too of the white T-shirts that men used to wear under their dress shirts. Once you had a few, you didn't need more until they wore out.

But is it true of silk-screened T-shirts? Perhaps not. This is not a utilitarian product. It's a fun product, one that people buy on impulse, because they feel like it.

133

And people who like T-shirts seem to buy a lot of them. While per capita ownership of T-shirts in this country is relatively low (less than five per person), some people own fifty or more shirts—and intend to keep on buying. If you survey college students, for example, you find that they own on average about twenty T-shirts and that they say they will probably buy five more in the next year. So it turns out that reversing the assumption about saturation is very helpful. It can lead you to useful insights into the market. And to the conclusion that sales shouldn't be slowing just because people in your local market already have lots of T-shirts. Something else must be the culprit.

For instance, perhaps you aren't offering enough new designs. Another thing that's different about T-shirts compared to many other products is that nobody owns two of the same design, just as nobody owns more than one copy of a book or CD they like. This can be turned into a great advantage, for to sell more T-shirts, all you have to do is offer lots of appealing new designs.

As you might have guessed, my recommendation was to scrap that four-city expansion plan and to replace it with a product-line expansion strategy instead. But I wouldn't have had the creative insight to "see" this alternative if I hadn't surfaced and then reversed a key assumption.

The Fault Pair Tree

PEAR TREE, PAIR TREE. GET IT? THAT play on words may not be the best, but it's useful for remembering and visualizing this method. Fault pair trees are good for doing **Why?** brainstorming for problems. They not only give you a way to organize the possible causes of a problem in a logical and visual pattern, but also help you think creatively about those causes so that you can gain insight into the problem and its solution.

HOW TO USE THE FAULT PAIR TREE

The Basic Method

Fault trees are not developed in a simple, linear method—they don't grow neatly and they require reworking over time. It's a creative process. Therefore the following steps are designed to get you started on the process, rather than to carry you all the way through it. With these steps and their explanations as guides, you can get familiar enough with fault pair trees to use them to your best advantage in creative problem solving.

135

The four basic steps are as follows:

❶ Write a clear and direct problem statement.

❷ Identify paired sets of faults or causes; use them to construct a fault pair tree.

❸ Ensure all pairs meet the requirement of completeness.

❹ Rework your fault pair tree in multiple passes.

Now for a closer look at each of these steps.

 ## Write a clear and direct problem statement.

How you define the problem will affect the quality of your fault tree. The more simple and direct, the better. Try a clear, action-oriented description of the problem, and avoid problem definitions with hidden causal assumptions in them. Remember, you will be focusing on causes in this method, brainstorming why the problem has occurred, and so you don't want anything "leading" (or misleading, as the case might be) in your statement.

➥ **For Example**

Let's say you turn on your computer and it doesn't start up. For your definition of the problem, you don't want to say, "The computer is broken," since that may not be why it won't go on. Instead, start with a description of

136

the actual problem as you experienced it, such as "The computer didn't start up when I flipped its switch from the 'off' to the 'on' position." That's all you really know about the problem, stripped of assumptions. If you condense that down, be careful not to lose or add anything significant to its meaning. It's fine to condense the statement to "The computer's switch doesn't turn the computer on," but not to "The computer's switch doesn't work," since your experience does not actually prove that statement to be true.

Perhaps the simplest and most direct description of the problem would be this one:

My computer won't turn on.

It gets the problem down to its bare essentials, does not suggest any assumptions that could mislead us, and so serves well as our problem statement.

 Identify paired sets of faults or causes; use them to construct a fault pair tree.

Once you have your statement, you're ready to construct a fault tree. As fault trees are represented visually, you'll need a large sheet of paper, a pencil, and an eraser—a big one, because over the course of working with your fault pair tree, you'll probably be doing a lot of erasing! Don't forget: this is a process that involves a good deal of revision.

To begin your fault pair tree, write your problem statement halfway down the right-hand side of the paper, and draw a box around it. Then identify a paired set of faults (or causes) that might explain why the problem has occurred. Write them next to the problem statement and box each one separately. Link them with a half circle or branching lines, to show they are paired; then connect them to the problem statement. Now brainstorm a paired set of faults (or causes) for each boxed fault. Write the pairs down, box them separately, link each set, and connect each set to its fault. Continue the process in this way, creating more "branches" for your tree.

➡ For Example

You might start by thinking "My computer won't turn on because it isn't getting power, or because of some internal problem." The first pair of faults are thus "no power to it" and "internal problem." You would draw boxes around them, link the boxes to show they are paired, and connect the set to what it explains: in this case, to "My computer won't turn on" (the "trunk" of the tree).

Next you might decide that "cord failed" and "cord unplugged" are two logical causes of the "no power to it" explanation. You would add these, linking them to indicate their relationship and connecting them to what they explain. And you might explain "internal problem" with another pair of alternatives. If you keep

EXHIBIT 6. Sample A, Fault Pair Tree

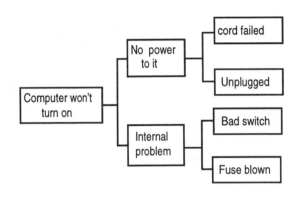

this analysis up long enough (and your technical knowledge holds out), you should eventually cover all the possible causes of your computer's failure to turn on. Exhibit 6 shows a simple tree based on this analysis.

Why expose all the possible causes? Because in problem solving, it's easy to overlook possible causes. Moreover, unless you sufficiently understand a problem's causes, you cannot hope to find a solution. Therefore creative thinking about problems needs to focus sharply on causality. And cause brainstorming—what you are really doing when you draw a fault pair tree—is a great way to gain creative insight into any problem.

139

3 Ensure all pairs meet the requirement of completeness.

Part of what makes the fault-pairs process complex is the requirement that you work in pairs. Here's a formal rule for how to do this:

Each fault pair must be *complete* at its level.

In other words, the pair must encompass **all possible explanations or causes**. This is obviously an artificial constraint. Why should there be only two causes? This kind of either/or thinking is quite limiting (and elsewhere in the guidebook I advise you to beware of it). But the interesting thing is, you can always find a way to encompass all possibilities using only two options. And the search for the right pair is inspiring, forcing considerable creative and analytical thinking. That's why I like to work within the constraint of a pairs-only fault tree. (Fault trees are often used in engineering and quality improvement contexts, but lack this constraint, and are more technical and less creative as a result.)

➥ For Example

Let's look again at Exhibit 6. Do the pairs in it meet the requirement of completeness? For instance, if there is no power to the computer, could this only be because of (1) a bad cord or (2) an unplugged cord? What if the computer is plugged into a surge protector, and that

140

isn't plugged in? Or maybe the surge protector and computer are plugged in, but the surge protector's switch is off or its fuse has blown. Maybe the computer cord and surge protector are fine, but the wall socket isn't receiving electricity. And why not? Is there a power outage, a circuit-breaker problem, or an electrician working on the wiring in the office? The more we think about this pair of faults, the more we can "see" new possibilities.

To encompass all these possible reasons for the computer not receiving power, I'd have to modify and expand my fault pair. In fact, I'd probably replace it with the far broader pair: (1) electricity not moving from wall switch to computer, and (2) electricity not reaching wall switch. Then I'd need to explore the numerous possible causes of each of these faults—again by building pairs that are complete at their level and encompass everything beyond them.

Another benefit of the paired-cause requirement is that it sometimes makes you think of a cause you wouldn't have considered otherwise, simply because you have to come up with something to round out a pair. The other day I had to diagnose what was wrong with a light in my office; it didn't work, and I didn't know why. Now this is a simple problem compared to a faulty computer, but I was stumped. So I tried a quick fault tree to stimulate my imagination. And it worked—I ended up struggling to find a second cause to go along with "bad light-bulb." Either a bulb is bad or good, I thought. What other fault could there be? For some reason I was plain "stuck" and couldn't see that a good bulb might simply have come loose in the socket. Only by staring at a blank spot in my fault tree was I able to come up with that cause. And in fact that **was** the cause of the problem. Exhibit 7 shows the fault tree I created.

 Rework your fault pair tree in multiple passes.

Fault pair trees are best designed through a series of "passes" in which you jot down your current best guesses, then revisit them later, probably replacing them with a new version. It usually takes three or four passes to get even a simple fault pair tree "right." It is therefore helpful to work on a large board or large sheets of paper, redrawing for each pass but keeping a copy of the old version in case you need it to jog your memory.

For example, in my first pass at the problem illustrated in Exhibit 7, my first pair of causes was "wall switch bad" and "light broken." But upon further thought, I saw this as an incomplete pair, and replaced it with "light is broken" and "no power reaching light." My mental script went something like this: "What if the light is unplugged or otherwise not getting power? Then these aren't a 'complete' pair of explanations."

EXHIBIT 7. Sample B, Fault Pair Tree

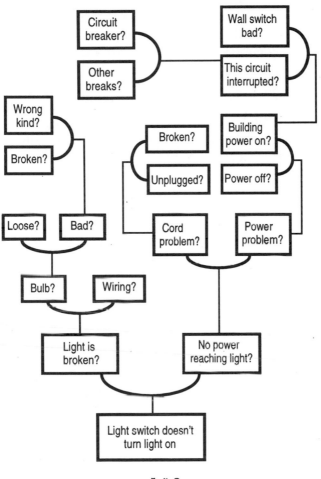

I didn't throw "wall switch bad" away, I just kept pushing it father down the branches of my growing fault tree until I found where it belonged. After several passes, it ended up four levels out—indicating that it was badly misplaced on my first pass and would have blinded me to many possible causes had I not revisited my thinking.

On my second pass, my mental script went like this: "It must be either no power to light or light not working (or both). OK, that seems complete, and I can try fitting more pairs into it." Then I went through several similar cycles of putting down pairs, and evaluating and rejecting them, before completing the tree in the Exhibit 7. (Note the alternative format used to draw the tree, which is built up from the bottom of the page—a possibility to keep in mind!)

What/How Thinking

THIS METHOD COMBINES several different thinking tools into a creative approach that is especially
suitable for designing "out-of-the-box" solutions to
problems. It helps you identify the components of the
problem and gets you started at moving them around
into novel configurations, so you have more material to
work with and can find new angles for attack. The
method does this in a peculiarly user-friendly way, by
having you begin with the benefits to the stakeholders:
customers, users, or whoever is affected directly by the
object or process in question.

In this respect, the method owes much to the field of
total quality management, and as you will see, it can
even be used to build that most powerful but esoteric of
TQM tools, the quality function deployment (QFD)
matrix. But you need not take it to that level to benefit
from it. There are many levels of What/How Thinking,
and the majority of applications do not require high-
level application. The "KISS" rule (Keep It Simple,
Stupid!) applies to this as to all creativity methods.

Because the method analyzes specific objects or processes, many people assume that its applicability is limited. Not so! Just about every subject of creativity can be defined as an object or process, even if you don't usually think of it that way. For instance, let's say you are wrestling with an interpersonal problem—perhaps a team has internal conflicts and the leader isn't good at resolving them. You could either take the object involved—the leader—as a subject for the method, or take the conflict resolution process itself. In fact, it could be helpful to do two analyses, one for each. You see, there is always some way to find an object or a process and make it the focus of your creative thinking. If you can't see at least one way to do so, stop and do some brainstorming on **that** problem first.

HOW TO USE WHAT/HOW THINKING

The Activity Steps

There are three major steps to this activity:

❶ Identify and explore the whats of the object or process.

❷ Identify and explore the hows related to the object or process.

❸ Build a What/How Relationship Matrix.

Identify and explore the whats of the object or process.

Whats are the things the object or process does, is supposed to do, or could do. They are its functions—what benefits an object or process delivers of value to its users. For example, a car door's functions include things like "protect occupant," "prevent theft," "keep external environment out," and "improve the look of the car."

The goal of this step is a lengthy and varied list of current and possible functions. Lots of whats. You can tackle this by simply brainstorming a list of functions. But it may not reveal as many possibilities as you need to form a creative solution. So here are additional techniques you can use during this step if necessary.

➡ **Brainstorm Using Function Questions**

Having trouble thinking of functions for your list? Then try posing and answering questions in these formats:

- "What are _____'s functions?"

- "What are all of _____'s possible uses or benefits?"

- "What can someone do with _____?"

Select a question and see how much easier it is to come up with a long and varied list of possible functions.

147

➥ Make a Function Tree

Instead of simply listing functions, map them by using lines to show which functions "nest" under which, thus creating a branching function tree. For example, in exploring a car door's functions, you would draw separate lines from "car door" to functions like "protect occupant" and "keep external environment out." Then you would show functions like "keep water out" and "keep sound out" as branching from "keep external environment out." Or, if you had listed some of these sub-functions first (functions don't always occur to you in nested order), you would identify their relationship, create the bigger category for them, and later go back and think of other sub-functions that fit in the category.

Your mental script might run like this as you work on the function tree:

The functions "keep water out" and "keep sound out" belong together, on a "keep external environment out" branch. And, let's see. Other functions on that branch include "keep wind out" and "keep criminals out." Hmm . . . is a robber part of the environment? Not the physical environment anyway. Maybe there's a bigger category, "Exclude," and one branch is "environment" and another is "people." That would suggest a similar branch, "include," with functions like "keep children in and people from falling out," "keep pets from jumping out," and "keep hot/cool air in." Do we offer any special restraints to keep pets safe and still allow them to get fresh air?

*And there are some things that the door neither excludes com-
pletely nor includes completely—at least, that's true of fresh
air, which the window lets in. And the view. So another main
category might be "Controlled Access to Environment." And
that includes "access to fresh air," "access to views," and,
hmm . . . anything else? "Access to toll booths." Wonder if
doors provide all the control we want for these functions? I
think we typically overlook this branch of the function tree.*

As you work with a function tree, the mental struggle to
group and nest functions forces many new **function ideas**
to the surface. Thus it's far easier to develop a lengthy
list of functions using a tree than a list. And many people find their mental scripts include a wide variety of
interesting new design concepts when they work with
function trees—as does the script above.

➡ **Explore Obvious and Non-Obvious Functions**

When you look at the functions of an object or process,
it's easy to stick with current functions—things that are
already part of the accepted deliverables. Car doors
are currently designed to do certain beneficial things for
us, and eventually your function tree should reveal all
of these obvious and accepted functions. But could car
doors do other things? Is it possible to put them to use in
the name of other, non-obvious or currently unacceptable functions? Sure. In general, there are alternative
functions, and it often helps to explore them too.

149

The simplest way is to brainstorm two lists of functions by dividing a sheet of paper or board into two columns, the first labeled "Obvious/Accepted Functions," the second labeled "Non-Obvious/Unaccepted Functions." The second category encourages freewheeling thoughts about odd and different uses for the object or process.

For instance, could a car door be used like a wing, to make the car fly? (No, but write it down anyway, as it might lead to something useful later.) Or could the door perform an entertainment function, instead of just sitting there, closed and immobile, while you drive? Actually, it already does, since speakers are often mounted on the door (but I wouldn't have thought of that without exploring the non-obvious). Could other forms of entertainment be added? Electronic game pan-els for back-seat doors? A pocket with protective flap, stuffed with fun road games? And so forth.

➡ **Combine the Function Tree and the Obvious/Non-Obvious Columns**

You can combine the above techniques by drawing your function tree on paper or board that's divided into two columns. This gives you the most support for creative thinking and is what I prefer when I use this method. I've illustrated the technique in Exhibit 8, in which I show a function tree for how to reduce complaints about lengthy elevator waits in an office building.

EXHIBIT 8. Elevator Function Tree

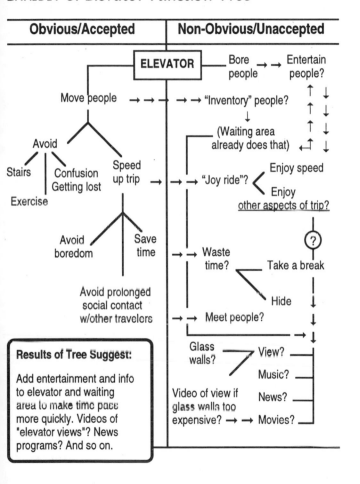

Obvious/Accepted	Non-Obvious/Unaccepted

Results of Tree Suggest:

Add entertainment and info to elevator and waiting area to make time pass more quickly. Videos of "elevator views"? News programs? And so on.

151

Sometimes you get what you want by working with the function lists and trees. If so, then stop here. But it's often productive to go on to Step 2, in which you move from thinking about **whats** to thinking about **hows**.

 Identify and explore the hows related to the object or process.

Attributes are the characteristics of the object or process in question, the things you are able to manipulate in designing it. They are often termed "hows" because they determine how you supply the whats, or functional benefits, of Step 1. The hows of car door design are things like the materials used, the nature of the door hinges, the handles, the weather stripping, and so on. An engineer who designs car doors can easily generate a lengthy, detailed list of hows, and even identify their formal measures (like weight, thickness, and closing pressure). The trouble with this engineering viewpoint is that it differs from the user's viewpoint. It isn't a functional perspective. Hows are the things we can manipulate to deliver desirable whats, but they aren't the whats, or functional benefits, in and of themselves. That's why What/How Thinking starts with a functional analysis rather than an attribute analysis.

But once you have some creative ideas about the whats, the functions you wish to deliver, then it is often helpful to explore the hows, the attributes you will use to deliver those functions. Furthermore, sometimes your analysis of hows leads to additional creative insights about whats (remember, the creative process is not linear). And so I recommend going through the same sort of analysis you used in Step 1, but focusing on attributes.

That means you need to brainstorm a list of hows. You may also find it useful to create a two-column list of obvious and non-obvious hows, and an attribute tree to explore the relationships among hows (the basic instructions are the same as those given in Step 1; just the focus is different). Take the attribute analysis as far as you need in order to gain creative insights and generate possible solutions to your problem.

Exhibit 9 illustrates a two-step analysis of the elevator problem, in which both functions and attributes of elevators are listed (see following page).

The display of whats and hows together should help you think of new and better ways to deliver the whats by using the available hows. But sometimes the design solutions still don't jump off the page—especially if you're dealing with a highly complex object or process, with lots of component whats. So you may want to go to the third step of What/How Thinking, in which you use a simplified version of the formal QFD grid or "House of Quality" matrix.

EXHIBIT 9. Analysis of Elevator Problem

ELEVATOR'S FUNCTIONS (WHATS)	
Obvious/Accepted	**Non-Obvious/Unaccepted**
Avoiding stairs	Meeting people
Getting to another floor quickly	Hiding
Avoiding unwanted social contact	Joy riding
Saving time	Giving you an opportunity for a short break
Avoiding exercise	Wasting time
Avoiding getting lost on the wrong floor	Boring you
	Entertaining you?

ELEVATOR'S ATTRIBUTES (HOWS)	
Obvious/Accepted	**Non-Obvious/Unaccepted**
Door(s)	Additional decorations?
Moving "room"	Ads?
Motor and mechanical stuff	Waiting area:
Light	Bells
Decorations (rugs, panels, mirrors)	Lighted buttons/indicators
	Seating?
Controls	Magazines?
Music	TV?
	TV/movies?
	View from window/clear walls?

③ Build a What/How Relationship Matrix.

Now comes the fun part. You get to draw a ridiculously large grid and start filling it up with strange symbols and notations. The idea is to look for creative ways of delivering the desired functional benefits (whats) from the hows. For instance, say that you have your design elements for the elevator-wait problem (like a waiting space with elevator buttons and lights, plus furniture and interesting items like wall hangings); how do you deliver these whats so that you get the most functional benefit from them? And is the list complete? Might adding something to do while people wait help reduce their boredom? And if you are going to provide things to do, what are those things and how can you deliver them using available hows? Or do you need to add some hows? Such are the questions that this step helps us cope with.

But first, take some time to create a neat grid, with room on both the left-hand side and at the top for row and column headings. Now enter your whats and hows in these spaces as headings. Whats go down the left-hand side, as row heads. That keeps them clearly in focus as your end goals. Hows go across the top, as column heads. If you have nested whats in a function tree and hows in an attribute tree, then you can try to maintain branch relationships by listing them in associated groups and by bracketing and labeling groupings. See Exhibit 10 for an example.

The exhibit is from a training course I wrote on Quality Function Deployment, a formal TQM method that uses such matrices for highly elaborate, involved design work. For complex objects or processes in which many factors interact and resource constraints frustrate the designers, I highly recommend the QFD process (it's absolutely great for reengineering complex processes). The steps I've described above, for What/How Thinking, are a great warm-up for QFD too. However, QFD is a lengthy and involved activity, requiring a commitment of many dozens of hours of work from a design team. And it takes some study to master—as you might imagine, since I wrote an entire training program on how to do it. So for most creativity efforts, my advice is, don't bother—a simpler process will probably serve your needs just as well.

Instead of using the matrix for a formal analysis of correlations between whats and hows—as QFD does— just use it for brainstorming. If you make the cells of your matrix big enough, you can write ideas in them, or big question marks with call-out code numbers to ideas and questions you list below the matrix. Thus, you're simply using the matrix as a visual aid for thinking about ways of delivering whats with hows.

EXHIBIT 10. What/How Relationship Matrix

			IMPORTANCE (Scale 12-9)	Door System Measurables							Lock System Measurables				
WHATs		**HOWs** →		Door Closing Effort O/S	Door Opening Effort O/S	Door Opening Effort I/S	Reach Dist. to Opening Mech.	Pull Force I/S	Dynamic Hold Open Force	Static Hold Open Force	Lock/Unlock Effort	Lock/Unlock Time	Key Insert Effort	Key Operating Effort	Freeze Resistance
		Column Number		1	2	3	4	5	6	7	8	9	10	11	12
1	Good Operation and Use	Easy to Open and Close	Easy Close from Outside	8												
2			Easy Open from Outside	2												
3			Easy Open Inside	4												
4			Easy Close from Inside	5												
5			Doesn't Kick Back	2												
6			Stays Open in Check Position	5												
7		Window Operates Easily	Crank Is Easy to Reach	6												
8			Crank Is Easy to Grasp/Hold	5												
9			Easy to Operate (Man.)	6												
10			Wipes Dry	4												
11			Operates Rapidly (Elec.)	2												
12		Lock and Latch Easily	Inside Lock Knobs Oper. Easily	6												
13			Key Operates Easily	6												
14			Doesn't Freeze	8												

Source: Alexander Hiam and Edward Feit, *Quality Function Deployment: Adding Value to Products and Processes*, American Management Association, Watertown MA, 1994, p. 82.

Don't be surprised if your analysis brings you back to earlier steps of the method. You may have a sudden idea that involves expanding on or reorganizing your lists of whats or hows. Great! The goal is creativity, not neatness, so go ahead and rework your matrix to reflect any and all ideas it generates. If need be, redraw it and start again. Pencils and chalk are cheap.

➥ Rating the Importance of Whats

To refine your work during Step 3, you can incorporate some survey data or best guesses about the relative importance of different whats. Exhibit 10 shows whats ranked by importance on a scale of 1 to 9, for example. The advantage of importance ratings is that they help you focus your design work on the whats or hows that the customers or stakeholders are most concerned with. And when there seems to be a trade-off decision, you can favor more important whats at the expense of less important ones. Just remember, you must rate the importance from the user's viewpoint, not the designer's.

Let's say, for example, that you want to gather data on the relative importance of various functions an elevator can provide to an office building's tenants. You might do this by making a list of the whats you've brainstormed, then asking tenants to rate each one on a 1 to 9 scale from unimportant to important. Also, you would have to be certain to leave a few lines labeled "Other" in case respondents can think of benefits that have escaped your notice. You might get some surprising answers that steer your work into more productive areas.

THE IMPORTANCE OF CUSTOMER VOICE

What/How Thinking developed from my work in TQM and process reengineering, both of which include a principle I find particularly applicable to creativity work. The principle is that you must **capture the customer's voice faithfully**. If you aren't familiar with TQM, this takes a bit of explaining. First, note that the customer is anyone who consumes or uses the object or process; in other words, customers are the stakeholders you're designing for—the people who care about the whats and will receive the benefits of your work. That means customers are not always paying customers—in fact, much of the time they aren't.

Second, note that the customer's voice is what those customers **say** about what they want, **in their specific language**. This is important even if they say stuff that sounds stupid or lacks technical knowledge of the object or process. You may know, for instance, that the time of an elevator trip is broken up into "call time," "egress time," "trip time," or some other set of technical terms people use in the elevator industry. But don't force your technical knowledge on the customer. Instead, listen to their voices and capture their way of thinking and talking about the wait. Maybe they divide wait time into "boredom," "embarrassment," "frustration," and "anxiety." If so, then you need to redesign the elevators to help users avoid those unpleasant emotional states, whether that involves cutting "egress time" or not!

The point is, the customer's **experience** of the object or process is captured in their voice. And their experience is the only reality that matters if you want them to be satisfied. That's why it's so important in quality work to listen carefully to what customers say and then to use their actual words faithfully throughout the creative design process.

➡ Customer Voice as a Creative Stimulus

What/How Thinking is at its most powerful as a creative tool when you carefully integrate customer voice into it. Just listen to people talk about your subject, or go and conduct some informal interviews with users or consumers. In many cases, you will be surprised by their views—and will learn new ways of "seeing" your subject from this exercise. And these views will help you write a fresh, new list of whats, which will stimulate many new, creative trains of thought. Customer voice can be a powerful stimulus of creative thinking, but only if you give it a chance.

160

13

Transferal: Creating a Climate for Creativity

WHETHER YOU ARE USING this guidebook for self-training or are basing a training curriculum on it, you face the same difficult issue everyone in training and development does: how to transfer what is learned to actual, practical use on the job. This issue is especially important in light of the generally accepted estimate that, of the whopping $400 billion in U.S. annual corporate training expenditures, only 10 percent transfers to profitable on-the-job changes in employee behavior. Apparently it's far easier to **learn** new skills and behaviors than to **use** them.

In this book, I've presented a new take on creativity that is designed to help break down these barriers between learning and using knowledge. My main strategy has been to give you more practical and powerful tools and techniques than are typically taught to trainees. This strategy helps close the learning-to-usage gap by delivering knowledge that is easier to use and more beneficial to use.

But the gap will still exist in your workplace, and in every other user's workplace, because there are many components to it, some of which I, the author, cannot eliminate. In the first chapter of this book, I shared the personal creativity assessment with you, which will help you identify factors that you can work on

"Welcome to your first staff meeting, Johnson. Since you're new, we thought you could suggest creative ideas for raising profits. And the rest of us will tell you what's wrong with them."

to maximize your creativity. And now, in this final chapter I'll share another perspective that may also be helpful to you.

TRANSFER CLIMATE AND ITS ASSESSMENT

Current research into the knotty problem of knowledge transfer in corporate training points to one particularly important but often overlooked set of factors; they concern the **transfer climate**—which I define as the context in which you try to use your knowledge. This context includes issues such as supervisor support (or lack of), peer support, opportunities to use the knowledge, and personal benefits arising from use of the knowledge. If all these forces are aligned to encourage us to use our new knowledge on the job, then we will use it. If not, we won't, and our training will be wasted.

Before ending this book, I want to help you take a careful look at the transfer climate in which your learning will (or will not) be applied. To do so, I have provided a simple but powerful assessment instrument you can use to anticipate both positive and negative influences and see whether the current transfer climate in your organization is favorable. The assessment also will help you find out which specific factors deserve your attention should the transfer climate be unfavorable.

We can often influence aspects of the transfer climate, whether we have positional power over them or not. Simply recognizing that a factor is holding us back is a big step toward fixing it. But unfortunately, most people fail to recognize the importance of transfer climate factors. So please, answer the following questions, and give some creative thought to improving your scores on any factors that you find are likely to block the successful use of newfound creativity skills. Remember: you will see more benefits from these skills if you identify the factors relevant to your workplace and do what you can to influence them in favor of the successful transfer of knowledge.

THE TRANSFER CLIMATE ASSESSMENT

Instructions: To evaluate the transferability of creativity skills in the workplace, check off all the items below that clearly apply to the workplace in question; then read the section on interpretation that follows.

✓ POSITIVE FACTORS

☐ Supervisors support and encourage use of learning about creativity on the job.

☐ Supervisors have a clear understanding of the learning and how it should be applied.

☐ People who use their creative skills in this workplace are likely to receive positive feedback concerning their efforts.

☐ If people know you are working on a creative effort, they are likely to offer their help and support.

☐ People who use their creativity skills in this workplace are likely to receive career benefits, such as raises or career advancement.

☐ People who use their creativity skills in this workplace are likely to receive recognition and rewards.

☐ People who make creative suggestions are kept well informed about the development of their ideas.

☐ Work provides frequent opportunities to use one's learning about creativity.

(Continued)

164

THE TRANSFER CLIMATE ASSESSMENT (Continued)

✓ MORE POSITIVE FACTORS

❏ Some of the most successful people in this workplace provide good role models of creativity and its value in work.

❏ Peers (including team members) agree that it is important to devote more time to creativity in the future.

❏ Supervisors will probably set goals concerning the use of creativity techniques.

✓ NEGATIVE FACTORS

❏ Most people in this workplace do not view creativity skills and behaviors as important.

❏ Supervisors discourage individual contemplation and creative thinking because they are not "physical" activities (people who do them look like they are goofing off).

❏ Peers sometimes discourage creative behaviors.

❏ The organization fails to provide resources needed to use creativity methods, such as appropriately equipped meeting rooms for group creativity and private places for individual creativity.

❏ Employees are sometimes penalized for making creative suggestions.

(Continued)

THE TRANSFER CLIMATE ASSESSMENT (Concluded)

✓ MORE NEGATIVE FACTORS

☐ It is often embarrassing to share one's most creative ideas in this workplace.

☐ People who use creativity skills in this workplace usually receive no feedback on their efforts.

☐ People who use creativity skills in this workplace are more likely to receive negative feedback than positive from their supervisor(s) and/or peers.

☐ People in this workplace cannot be trusted with one's potentially embarrassing ideas and information.

➡ Interpretation of the Assessment

The good news is this. If you checked off even a few of the positive factors, your transfer climate has some strongly beneficial elements. These are factors that will encourage you (or those you train) to actively apply creativity skills at work. Even one positive factor can make a big difference. And it isn't too hard to build the number of good influences.

Use the eleven items in the "Positive" category as a basis for your planning by looking for factors you can add to the mix. If you tackle the factors one at a time, you can often add four or five without too much resistance. I bring up resistance because you will certainly need to enlist the help of others—supervisors, peers, team leaders, and so forth—so be prepared to educate them about the importance of these positive factors. Think of creative ways to convince and remind them that they need to encourage the use of creativity in order to profit from it.

The bad news is this. If you checked off any of the nine negative factors, you can expect some serious obstacles to profitable use of creativity skills. Any one of these factors is capable of sabotaging the transfer of creativity skills. Unlike the positive factors, they aren't easy to deal with. You can't, for example, just eliminate one or two and expect to see a big improvement. That's because we are all pretty sensitive about creative behaviors—and quick to "pull in our creative heads" if the climate is unfavorable or threatening in any way.

So to really profit from creativity, you need to work systematically on the negative factors, with the goal of eliminating them all as soon as possible. Seriously! And you will find considerable difficulty in doing so. Difficulty arises from three sources:

1. Your own bad habits. Are you sufficiently aware of them to change them?

2. Others' bad habits. Make sure you build awareness of negative behaviors so people will be able to "catch themselves" before engaging in those behaviors.

3. Others' resistance. Some people just won't buy the idea that creativity is vitally important. You better be prepared to sell the idea to them, or they will secretly sabotage the transfer climate by behaving negatively toward those who try to be creative. The best way to sell people on the value of creativity is to get them to study it too!

Forewarned is forearmed. Plan to work on breaking your own and others' bad habits, and also expect some active resistance from those who don't yet understand the value of creativity.

But even with this knowledge and preparation, you may be unable to eliminate all nine negative factors. Don't despair! The alternative is to balance them with a larger number of positive factors. We all recognize that the workplace is never ideal, and as long as there are enough positive factors to make us feel that creativity is accepted and beneficial, we can learn to live with the occasional negative response.

When you act creative, you **are** creative. But when you act creative, some people think you're nuts. Hey, you can live with that. It comes with the territory. Trust me, the payoff in great new ideas is worth far more than the occasional embarrassment.

TO RECAP:
Process Tools and Transferal

These are the creative process tools and transferal material we have covered in Part 2. They will get you started on nurturing your creative greenhouse and helping others do the same. Good luck, and again . . .

| **May the force of creativity be with you!** |

🌀 The Creatercize Activity

🌀 The Magic Toolbox

🌀 Three-Step Word Association

🌀 Category Expansion

🌀 Surfacing Assumptions

🌀 The Fault Pair Tree

🌀 What/How Thinking

🌀 Transferal: Creating a Climate for Creativity

Index

NOTES

NOTES

NOTES

NOTES

NOTES

NOTES

NOTES